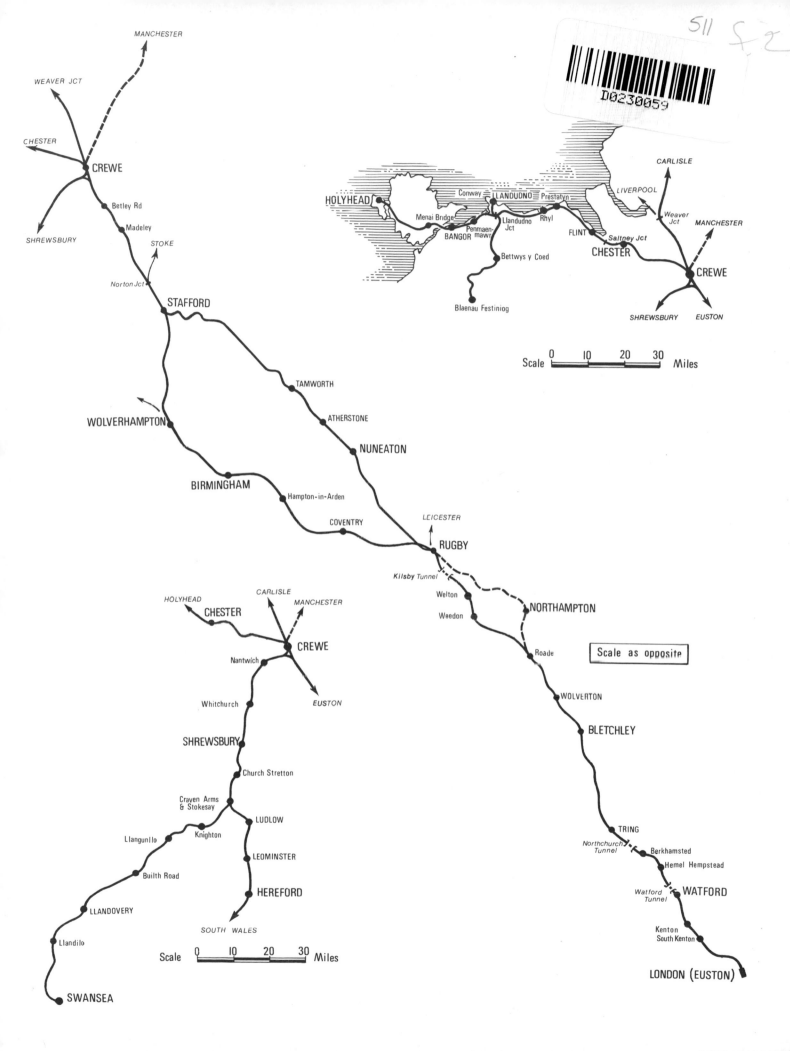

MANCHESTER

WEAVER JCT

CHESTER

CREWE

Betley Rd

Madeley

SHREWSBURY

STOKE

Norton Jct

STAFFORD

TAMWORTH

ATHERSTONE

WOLVERHAMPTON

NUNEATON

BIRMINGHAM

Hampton-in-Arden

COVENTRY

LEICESTER

RUGBY

Kilsby Tunnel

Welton

NORTHAMPTON

Weedon

Roade

Scale as opposite

WOLVERTON

BLETCHLEY

HOLYHEAD

CARLISLE

MANCHESTER

CHESTER

CREWE

Nantwich

EUSTON

Whitchurch

SHREWSBURY

Church Stretton

Craven Arms
& Stokesay

LUDLOW

Llangunllo
Knighton

LEOMINSTER

Builth Road

HEREFORD

LLANDOVERY

SOUTH WALES

Llandilo

Scale   0   10   20   30   Miles

SWANSEA

TRING

Northchurch
Tunnel
Berkhamsted

Hemel Hempstead

Watford
Tunnel
WATFORD

Kenton
South Kenton

LONDON (EUSTON)

HOLYHEAD

Conway
LLANDUDNO
Prestatyn

CARLISLE

LIVERPOOL

Menai Bridge

Llandudno
Jct
Rhyl

Weaver
Jct

MANCHESTER

BANGOR
Penmaen-
mawr

FLINT

Saltney Jct

Bettwys y Coed

CHESTER

CREWE

Blaenau Festiniog

SHREWSBURY   EUSTON

Scale   0   10   20   30   Miles

Roaming the
West Coast Rails

Roaming the West Coast Rails

DEREK CROSS

LONDON

IAN ALLAN LTD

First published 1980

ISBN 0 7110 0998 8

© Ian Allan Ltd 1980

Published by Ian Allan Ltd, Shepperton, Surrey,
and printed by Ian Allan Printing Ltd at their works
at Coombelands in Runnymede, England

Contents

To the memory of Eric Treacy who taught more of my
generation about railway photography than we realise,
or care to admit: and who was also a very great friend.

Preface

The dictionary definition of the term 'Roaming' is to ramble, to wander about, to change about inconsistently. To ask a railway photographer to compile a book of pictures under the general heading of 'Roaming' is putting temptation in his way, as at heart those of us who have looked on the railway as an aesthetic subject are all wanderers. We tend to go where our fancies take us, or where the wind and weather force us. Yet time and again we return to where our work or appreciation of a landscape appeals to us. There is often a difference and this book shows it well. My whole inclination is to the high wide open spaces, the Shaps and Llangunllos. My son, to whom I am greatly indebted for much of the modern motive power part of this book, by the nature of his work found himself in the 'Coronation Street' country of Lancashire and the 'Black Country' of Birmingham. This involved not only the generation gap, but a geological gap depending on where we cut our railway photographic teeth. In the case of this book the much talked of and greatly exaggerated generation gap emotionally did not exist as we each knew a good or a bad photo taken by the other and did not hesitate to praise or condemn. Where it did exist to our mutual advantage was that David saw the end of steam grow into the diesel and electric era and adapted accordingly. On the other hand I saw the end of steam degenerate into an era of similar looking biscuit boxes that moved me hardly at all. My one over-riding criterion being that diesels, like people, look better with noses. I am still of the opinion that the best looking of all British diesels were the original LMS 'Twins' No 10000 and 10001, significantly designed by a man steeped in steam. The old mariners adage that those brought up under sail made better officers on steam ships may well have carried into the steam/diesel transition in the case of engineers. The first generation diesels had a character whereas their successors have more and more become glorified cake tins. Only with the influence of the aircraft industry in such things as the HST, or that electric eel the APT, has modern railway traction regained something of an individual character: though I still have some doubts about the concept of an integral train.

What I call the geological gap is harder to define. Put bluntly this is probably due to my distaste for my fellow men in bulk and the works they have created. There are many factories but few Chatsworths... Coronation Streets outnumber Regent Streets by a depressingly large margin.

A curlew at Grayrigg I find infinitely more interesting than a factory at Farrington, a stone wall on Shap more pleasing than a block of council houses in Wigan. These are my own tastes I admit as they all have their uses. My geological training must have a bearing on this, but this said, I have to admit that it is a great deal easier to compose a picture in the once empty spaces of the Lune Gorge than amidst the teeming industrial landscapes of Birmingham. The two concepts are wholly different and here in a strange way modern power comes into its own. Diesels and electrics seem far more a part of a densely populated landscape than a steam locomotive ever did. I know that it was the Industrial Revolution that gave railways and steam locomotives their birth, though in many cases it was the chicken and the egg syndrome, with no clear demarcation as to which inspired what to the greater extent. Somehow a diesel or electric locomotive looks at home among the houses and factories of industrial Britain... out in the wilds of the high Pennines or Scottish hills it seems a pathetic lost soul. Similarly a steam locomotive throwing smoke and cinders on to the high fells and shouting its defiance at the empty spaces of the hills, with only the sheep to answer, is right. Man challenging nature in an obvious if inefficient way. I will admit that for 125 years steam engines climbing Shap were a gross waste of effort, but they looked and sounded as if they were overcoming something worth tackling. Electrics go up far faster and

Above: The extraordinary quality of the light on Shap, even on a showery day shows to advantage in this picture of a newly built 'Clan' No 72001 *Clan Cameron* at Shap Wells in July 1952 with the morning Manchester-Glasgow express. The fact that No 72001 is tackling Shap with 13 coaches un-assisted says a lot for their hill climbing ability, something much appreciated by the Carlisle men. In retrospect the 'Clans' were considered a failure, but they were never given a fair trial, and many drivers I have spoken to, who had to work them over hilly roads, maintained that properly fired they were sure footed and strong on the banks.

with far less waste of energy, but they don't belong.

Modern motive power needs a complex background as it lacks character. A beautiful woman in an empty room still makes you stop and stare, a plain woman needs an interesting background to be noticed at all. This may be an over-simplification, but it has been said that there has never been a really ugly steam engine, though the old North Eastern had some very good tries. The phrasing of this is wrong, there have been ugly steam engines but there has never been one without character; no matter how bad that character may have been as in some of Webb's more elaborate experiments in compounding. This brings me back to where I started: the term 'Roaming'. 'To ramble, to wander about, to change inconsistently' . . . it may be fun but it does

not make a book. To write a book without a central theme is like the world in the time of Genesis . . . it is without form and void. The temptation is strong and like Oscar Wilde I tend to be able to resist anything except temptation, so have settled that *Roaming the West Coast Rails* be confined to the lines of the old London and North Western Railway. This is a supreme piece of hypocrisy as it happens, as the old LNW could resist anything but the temptation to trespass on somebody elses territory so I have left myself a fairly wide field. In conclusion I would like to thank my son David for putting his extensive collection of dull diesels in duller places at my disposal to give a far more comprehensive geographical coverage in this book than I could have managed on my own. The photos in these areas are his, the faults in the captions my own.

Introduction

*Both flowers and weeds spring when sun
is warm,
and Great Men do great good . . . or else
great harm'*
Webster 'The White Devil'

This book is a photographic essay on the
lines of the old London & North Western
Railway. Not in its glory, as it was
absorbed in to the LMS some years
before I was born, though I have been
lucky enough to travel behind, and for a
short distance on, the immortal
Hardwicke, surely the best known and in
many ways the most historical of all
Britain's wealth of preserved engines. My
opening quotation was the fascination of
the old LNW with its black engines and
often black hearted men who ran it. It
called itself the 'Premier Line' and had as
its coat of arms Britannia, a more or less
replica of the Royal Arms, known to the
men as the 'cauliflower', which lingered
far into the LMS days as the nickname of
a class of undoubtedly very remarkable
goods engines. It has bequeathed to
posterity some of the most remarkable if
terrifying martinets of Victorian and
Edwardian commercial life, Huish, Moon,
and above all Francis Webb, whose
name hangs over the great Crewe Works
even today with the cold awesomeness
of freezing fog. This same Crewe Works
were mainly of Webb's creation, as was
the town they took their name from, but
by the same token they produced some
of the greatest locomotive engineers in
this or many other countries. They also
produced some very remarkable engines
which with the perversity of modern
history are forgotten in the near misses
of some of Webb's compounds. It was
without doubt a highly efficient railway
backed by equally efficient if buccaneer-
ing commercial acumen. I would have
liked to have been one of its major
shareholders just as I would equally have
disliked being its neighbouring rival
railway. I would also have been chary of
being a partner in anything in contact
with it, especially in the Welsh borders or
north-west England. Geologically and
from a social historical point of view it
has in its line from London to Carlisle the
most interesting main line in Britain and
possibly the world. This line had some of
the finest scenery in England and also
some of the worst . . . the sulphurous
caverns of Liverpool and the high windy
uplands of Shap, the gracious rolling
country of the shires and the coal-
besmirched slums of Wigan. Everything
about the old LNW was contradictory . . . there were no half measures
about it. It was either brilliant or bloody
awful, depending I suppose on whether
you travelled on the crack 'Corridor'
express from London to Glasgow or
some of the less creditable local trains in
West Cumberland.

There is one very interesting fact
about the London & North Western . . . it
is the best known pre-Grouping railway
in Britain, far from its native shores.
Many times in far away places railway
enthusiasts have told me that they would
have given their soul to see a LNW
express in full cry on Shap or bursting
out of Kilsby Tunnel. This to an
Englishman is strange, as we had all
been subconsciously conditioned to
accept that the Great Western *was*
England at best, to all who had not faced
its Cornish branch lines in our youth. This
is not so for to many friends in America,
Australia, New Zealand and other far
away places with high sounding names,
to them, it was the London & North
Western that summed up British railways
before the 1923 Grouping. The Great
Western was a very English thing, in
some cases Elgar, but more often
Vaughan Williams . . . a line of military
Pomp and Circumstance but in its more
charming bye-ways the scent of cider
orchards and the unique red soils of
Devon. Just what the mystique of the old
LNW was I can't be sure, its parentage
from the Liverpool and Manchester may
have had something to do with it. Its
roaring fire throwing glistening black
engines certainly had . . . Webb got his
sums right long before Henry Ford when
he said 'I will paint my engines any
colour you like so long as it is black'. Sir
William Stanier will be remembered

above all for his 'Black Five' 4-6-0s . . . would he have been remembered as well for them had they been green? Undoubtedly the race of fierce martinets that controlled its destinies will linger in railway lore far longer than many of their equally able if less domineering contempories. This may be the real reason why the London & North Western holds such a fascination in international railway history. In late Victorian times people expected the captains of big British companies to be fiercesome tyrants and the LNW certainly had its share. In retrospect it was extraordinarily well served by its civil engineers the two most notable of which were Joseph Locke and Robert Stephenson whose work I will deal with later.

This book falls into five sections both through their original ownership and the country they served. This is a very broad subdivision but the whole five are joined to the spine of the great main line from London to Carlisle and as this is a mirror of the whole LNW lines I can do no better than set the scene by describing a trip over this line. The interesting fact about this being that it was not made in the days of steam but in August 1978 on the 16.45 Euston-Glasgow express behind a prosaic Class 86/2 electric No 86.245. Yet for all this the meteorological conditions and a series of very determined drivers made it a trip of high drama and one that showed the great LNW main line in all its many faces. The start out of Euston while probably more interesting from a railway engineering point of view has never been as spectacular as that from the neighbouring Kings Cross but on this sultry afternoon in August with more than a hint of thunder in the air it was impressive none the less. The Camden Bank is never to be treated lightly, a legacy from the days of rope haulage when Euston was first opened. Still we made a promising enough start and by Harrow were probably up to the permitted 100mph, the remarkably rural north London suburbs passed by in the gloom of this sultry afternoon. There was a long permanent way restriction at Berkhamsted which I had expected and assumed would cause delays on the way. Then two things happened, the sun came out through towering cumulus clouds and it became obvious that the driver was out to get to Preston (the first stop) on time if he could. The lighting conditions were extraordinary and I began to take notice of the landforms we passed through and the way they had been tackled 140 years before; for while electrification had altered the line in detail, Robert Stephenson's original layout remains virtually as it was built.

The great cuttings such as Tring and Roade were all the more dramatic, lit by a lowering sun reaching through the thunderclouds, the great sweeping embankments striding across the rolling country of the Midlands dappled in sunshine and showers. The alien mess of Milton Keynes emphasising that the art of civil engineering has not improved within the last century and a quarter. It was not hard to imagine myself on the footplate of *Adriatic* or *Jeanie Deans* bucketing northwards some 70 years before until you realised that the train I was on was probably doing 100mph most of the way. It is at Rugby that the first of the many changes on the London-Carlisle line became apparent, not in the nature of the landscape which until Stafford remains typical of the rolling shires of middle England, but in the nature of the line. The great earthworks are gone and the Trent Valley line is relatively featureless but in many ways is one of the most interesting sections of the West Coast route to the north, as it was here that the two engineering talents of Locke and Robert Stepehsnon worked in closest collaboration. On my trip of August 1978 it was here that what had been a threat of thunder turned into a reality, with violent thunderstorms alternating with periods of that uniquely clear sunshine so common after a storm. The severity of these storms was brought vividly into perspective by the sight of two up expresses standing cheek by jowl in Colwich station, the lightning having apparently knocked out the signalling between there and Lichfield. It was an apt reminder that in any conflict between man and nature the latter often holds the ace. The northward journey from Crewe was equally interesting as the thunderstorms with the low westerly sun lit up the whole of the south Lancashire plains against a backdrop of storm-wracked hills and made rain-washed Warrington look like Canaletto's Venice — well not quite, but certainly different from any other time I have seen Warrington.

The London men left the loco at Preston after what had been a brilliant run under far from ideal conditions. Preston in the best traditions of that place managed to delay the departure for a few minutes and then the final chapter of this spectacular run began. By Lancaster it was getting dusk and while the low sun still lit the flats along the coast to Carnforth the hills ahead were an inky black. This was the most dramatic transition of all: the weather coinciding with the geography to show the change between the relatively easy miles that had gone before, and the final 60-mile struggle through the fells and over Shap to Carlisle. I have been over Shap many times in trains and walked it many more, but I have never known anything like that evening. As we sped through the Lune Valley it got darker and darker, until you could have sworn that the darkness could be felt, then above Tebay the storm broke with one of the most vivid displays of lightning I have ever seen in England. No wonder Shap became a household word in railway difficulties. We topped the summit still well into the 60s but one couldn't help thinking what it must have been like on the half covered footplate of a 'Jumbo' half a century before. The dying embers of the sun lit us into Carlisle but it had been an elemental journey on an elemental line. The shades of Moon and Huish must have been laughing in Valhalla.

Why should somebody born in Kent, living a good part of his life abroad and now in exile in Caledonia have such an obsession with the lines of the old LNW? A trite answer would be that much of my professional geological career was connected with volcanoes and from all I have read or seen the locomotives of the LNW were probably the nearest thing to a man made volcano yet invented! This is not true, unless there is some hidden Freudian significance that I have missed. The real reason was a book published by Ian Allan in 1952 called *Steam Up* by the late Eric Treacy and which cost in those halcyon days 10s/6d (52½p) in proper money . . . long before the decimal confetti of today was ever dreamed of. In my mind for anyone's money of any kind *Steam Up* is probably the best book of railway photographs ever published, ranging as it did from the cavernous cuttings of Liverpool to the curlew calling heights of Shap. In those days I had no way of getting to walk the perils of Olive Mount or the Lime Street tunnels but I could go to Shap. What is more my elderly Zeiss 116 camera would not have taken kindly to the lights and shadows of Lime Street as 116 film was a dying breed and available only in rather slow Orthochromatic emulsion. Moreover its elderly and arthritic shutter was not up to coping with the steam hauled expresses of these days in full cry just as my elderly and arthritic limbs find it hard to cope with modern electric hauled equivalents. The solution then was Shap where heavy postwar trains were worked hard and slowly but in very spectacular surroundings. A 16-coach train struggling to the Summit on a good day was within the camera's capabilities given sunshine and a good deal of luck. There were other considerations. My somewhat elderly Series E Morris could normally manage the 250-mile return trip from Ayrshire to Tebay without expiring completely. Even if it did, the whole journey could be done by train and I have on several occasions bought a ticket from Tebay to Kilmarnock with LNW/G & SW overprinted with LMS which in turn, was altered to BR.

Another source of transport to Shap if you were staying at Tebay was the local postmen who were more than ready to supply lifts in their vans on their visits to isolated farms. Often one could hitch a lift back on a banker. This was the astonishing thing about Shap in the early 1950s everyone was so friendly. The railwaymen were interested in what you were doing and went out of their way to help you. My classic example of this was when a returning banker and length of rope removed an irritating broom bush near Shap Wells by the simple method of attaching one end of the rope to the broom bush, the other to a buffer then letting the brake off... the rope being returned to the neighbouring farmer who was much amused by the whole proceeding. I suppose that it was this friendliness of the men that has made Shap so much my photographic home as will be seen all too clearly in this book. What is more it has been a lasting friendship in many cases as I still have contacts with many of the railwaymen who worked there while I was at University in 1950/51. Like all good things it couldn't last and by the end of steam some 17 years later the railwaymen had had enough of hordes of railway enthusiasts whose whole manners and approach to the hobby had changed from that of harmless eccentricity to football style hooliganism. Yet it is a memory that has lingered and coloured my approach to the lines of the old LNW more perhaps than anything else. What is more it cropped up all over the system, the men were proud of their company and its great traditions and welcomed anyone who took an intelligent interest in it. One of the best alfresco lunches I have ever eaten was prepared by a signalman on the Central Wales line much to my embarrassment, simpy as I had made a rude remark about the Great Western. Even in the dying hours of steam an inspector at Carlisle who was far too young even to have seen the old LNW in action remonstrated with me for photographing a train about to go over the Midland.

What was the reason for the inate friendliness of the men who ran the lines of what was once the London & North Western? It wasn't only on the Lancaster & Carlisle it was over the whole system... show an interest and you were shown what you wanted to see. Even a very bedraggled raw RAF recruit was once shown over Crewe Works! I suspect that it stemmed from an inbred sense of superiority... it was the Premier Line and aristocrats are always more approachable men than say trade union officials, their's is a pride to be displayed and not a false pride that may be destroyed by a discerning observer. One last story of the LNW in BR days must suffice but it tells a lot. Not surprisingly it happened on the Lancaster & Carlisle section but could equally well have happened anywhere else. It was my custom to go to the Shap area on the peak Glasgow Fair holiday weekends and on one Thursday I arrived from the south and so did not have the chance to contact my various friends from Carlisle southwards. Late in the evening I called in at Oxenholme to see if there was anything interesting running the following day. Having got my information I asked who was on which shift and where. I was then told that Charlie R. was on at Penrith No 1 (now like all the other characteristic LNW boxes on that line demolished). Now Charlie, like many of the signalmen in the fell country, had a small holding where he kept a few pigs and some sheep and I spoke to him on the railway phone. The price of pigs came up and several other farming topics when the conversation was interrupted by Carlisle Control with a rich Cumbrian voice saying sternly 'Charlie if you and that Mr Cross want to discuss the price of pigs, get him to buy a pint in a pub, but get off the railway phone, there's been a derailment at Hest Bank'. The irony of this being that nobody was in the least surprised that the railway phone on one of the busiest main lines in the country was being used to discuss the price of pigs.

In laying out this book I have stuck as

closely as possible to the original companies that finally came to make up the London & North Western. Three are obvious choices. The London & Birmingham, the Grand Junction and the Lancaster & Carlisle with their appropriate branches. The other two sections are more fluid and classed as Welsh incursions and North Lancashire. The Welsh section is reasonably straightforward but the early history of the north Lancashire lines most certainly is not. These generalised sections fall into a geographical and to a lesser extent a geological entity. They also highlight the different approaches of two very eminent early civil engineers, Robert Stephenson and Joseph Locke. Much has been made of the row between Locke and George Stephenson over the Grand Junction but this animosity did not exist between Robert Stephenson and Locke, who were to remain friends and professional confidantes throughout their spectacular if relatively short careers, both men dying young. Robert Stephenson responsible for the London & Birmingham, and Chester & Holyhead lines favoured the theory that the shortest distance between two points was a straight line, especially if it could be kept relatively level. Locke on the other hand believed in using every trick that natural landforms could give him even if it entailed stiffer grades and slightly longer distances. The result of this difference in approach was that Robert Stephenson has left behind some very impressive memorials in the form of bridges and tunnels. Locke on the other hand despite some very impressive viaducts south of Warrington on the Grand Junction has left few major structural works and as far as the scope of this book is concerned virtually no tunnels at all. I will elaborate on these points in the introductions to the various sections, which while not in any way being a definitive history of the lines illustrated is an attempt to show the varying nature of the area served by the LNW and the type of influence the railway had on these areas. The latter however is a near impossibility as nobody has really answered the key question. Did the coming of the railways being about the full flood of the Industrial Revolution or was it the other way about. It is the chicken and the egg syndrome . . . which came first?

In compiling this book I have deliberately tried to give as wide a coverage of locomotive classes, places and other items of railway interest as possible. In some instances this had led to having to use old negatives that may not be up to modern Press camera standards. For all this I feel I am justified, as it is not 'my hundred best photographs'. all of which would probably be on Shap. It is an attempt to show the West Coast rails as I know them in the last decade of steam and in the transition to more modern forms of power. I can only ask that my imperfections be treated as an essential part of the whole picture.

The London & Birmingham

A very great deal has been written of the history of this line which was among the very first main lines to the capital. Even more has been written about its grandiose Doric Arch and gatehouses, torn down in the last decade — an act of wanton vandalism masquerading under the name of progress. When the first stage of the London & Birmingham was opened in 1837, these splendid structures hid a rather mean two-platformed station known rudely as a 'train barn', from whence trains were hauled up as far as Chalk Farm by means of an endless rope, the same device being used to guide trains into the terminus. The reason for this steep initial incline out of Euston was to get under the Regents Canal, canals as we will see later being the bane of many of the LNW constituents formative years. This elaborate facade hiding a less than remarkable structure was also a feature of the original Curzon Street terminus of the L&B and such contrasts were somehow perpetuated throughout the West Coast main line's history even into BR days. I remember vividly in 1951 the three-coach portion of the 'Lakes Express' arriving at Penrith behind an immaculate 'Duchess' to be taken forward to Keswick by a 75-year old Webb 'Cauliflower' goods engine! From its stark beginnings Euston, like Topsy, 'just growed' though such things as rope worked inclines had long since departed. In its ultimate development before and after the war the 'old' Euston was a fascinating place, dark, smokey and full of character and yet it seemed to work, other than what appeared to be a mandatory stop on the Camden Bank for incoming sleeping car expresses. Occasionally outgoing sleeping car expresses took a bit of finding, especially if there was a hint of fog abroad, a fog which seemed to penetrate the minds of officialdom as well as the atmosphere. Still it had a certain grim charm and was at least all on the level. With the coming of electrification all this has changed and is certainly not on the level as anyone with a damaged ankle soon realises. It lacks charm even if trains seem to arrive and depart on time, and has succumbed to the mania among modern architects that to get from A to B it is necessary to climb at least one flight of stairs and then down another finishing up the same height above ordnance datum as you were when you started. Efficient it may be, but a place to linger in and ponder history certainly not. Not that one is given encouragement to do so as there are no seats in what I am told is known as a 'circulating area'. I remonstrated to an inspector one evening about this and got the astonishing reply 'Well sir if we put seats here people would sit on them!' Presumably we should circulate.

The initial climb out of Euston is remarkable for a series of burrowing junctions enabling empty stock and light engines to be got to and from the terminus without fouling any of the main running lines. This network of tunnels I have never really understood despite studying diagrams, seeing them from the footplate and even being taken on a conducted tour of them, or part thereof. The fact is that they work rather well and there was never the congestion at Euston that there was at Kings Cross while getting engines and coaches in and out of platforms. To a degree such movements were alleviated at peak times by stock brought in for one train by a locomotive booked for a following one at an adjacent platform. These engines would give the departing trains a hefty shove in the rear as far as the platform end and then drop back for their own workings. With electrification this has changed and Class 87s and 86s glide noiselessly on their way. I nearly said without fuss, but the first time I left Euston in the cab of an electric the driver had to do some very dexterous work with the controls in response to several determined efforts to slip on Camden Bank. Once clear of the Camden-Willesden complex comes one of the most surprising features of the London & Birmingham. Of all the great main lines out of London it is the quickest to come into relatively rural scenery. Beyond Wembley trees and parks are as much a part of the landscape as rows of suburban houses, unlike many of the other lines into London industry seems remarkably lacking. An interesting feature of the initial gradually rising 15 miles to Bushey is the presence on the down side of the joint LMR/London Transport electrified lines with their two conductor rails. Until the steep cutting at Bushey, long famed as the site of the first of many sets of water troughs on the WCML, there are no earthworks of note and no grade (apart from the Camden Bank) steeper than 1 in 339, very modest in terms of the other main lines from London to the north. Beyond Watford the line tunnels through the first of several ridges lying transversely from south-west to north-east across its path.

It is hard to see how Robert Stephenson could have avoided this ridge north of Watford other than by a precipitous cutting, and it is significant that when the line came to be quadrupled some years later tunnelling was again resorted to. The initial double track Watford tunnel gave considerable trouble with quicksands and water in its construction and should have been a warning of what could, and did follow. Significantly the quadrupling of some of the tunnels on the line subsequently took the form of two single bores. Beyond the Watford Tunnel the line continues climbing on very easy grades through wooded gently rolling country and places like Kings Langley and Berkhamsted, still remarkably unspoiled in this age of urban sprawl. It is on this length that the main line is joined by the

Grand Union Canal which is to keep it company for much of the way to Rugby. The summit of this initial gradual climb out of London comes at Tring immediately followed by the long and deep Tring cutting which is one of the more spectacular features of the line between London and Birmingham. Apart from the Watford Tunnels, which I don't think could have been avoided, it is Tring that marks the L&B as a Stephenson line. The chalk ridge of Tring could have been circumvented and I feel Locke probably would have done so, but Robert Stephenson liked to keep things straight and so went through it. Fortunately the strata was stable and for all its depth Tring cutting gave little trouble, if great labour in its construction, but has been little trouble since.

North of Tring the countryside becomes less wooded open arable land with the only town of any importance being Bletchley, at one time an important junction but with the closing of many lines in the Beeching epoch now of less importance from a railway point of view. It is now in danger of being enveloped in the amorphous mess of Milton Keynes. The next place of any significance is Wolverton. In the early days of both the London & Birmingham and later the LNW this was a place of considerable railway importance being the locomotive shops of the London & Birmingham, and until the completion of Crewe of the Southern Division of the infant LNW. Engines were often changed here and a refreshment stop provided for the passengers, by all accounts the catering was just about as good as the equivalent establishment at Swindon of the same epoch was bad. Wolverton is now one of

Below: A view of the 'New Euston' not long after the inauguration of the full electrification to Liverpool and Manchester with everything looking new and clean. The photo shows No E3139 then classified AL6 subsequently renumbered 86.043 on 1S75 the last afternoon express to Glasgow and another AL6 No E3147 on a Manchester train. At this time all the LMR electrics were fitted with raised chrome numbers which when kept clean were a marked improvement on the painted ones of today.

the main carriage works of BR as it was for the LMS, and stabling point for the Royal Train when not in use.

Wolverton is an interesting example of how busy and important railways were to become, the volume of traffic far exceeding the expectations of the early engineers. The various works grew up higgledy-piggledy on either side of the original main line causing considerable congestion to all and sundry. Thus, when it became obvious that the main lines out of Euston would have to be quadrupled, a completely new line was built to the east of the original town and works but so well laid out that modern trains scarcely slacken speed taking this deviation. Eight miles north of Wolverton at Roade the line again enters a deep cutting which contains the junction for the Northampton loop, a railway layout spectacular to look at but nearly impossible to photograph. Much has been written about the reason why North-ampton was not on the original London-Birmingham main line as at that time, with the possible exception of Coventry, it was the most important town between the two cities. Some sources say that the townspeople did not want the railway others that certain landowners raised objections. My own feeling is that Robert Stephenson having been commissioned to build a railway between London and Birmingham resolved on the shortest possible course. Little did he know what this held in store for him. However in the event the main line set its sights northwards and Northampton was bypassed though subsequently served by a branch from Blisworth until the loop was opened 20 years later. Another change takes place at Roade for, while the line has been quadrupled as far as there, with the divergence of the Northampton lines it becomes double track from there to Rugby. From Roade to Welton is one of the great racing stretches of the London & Birmingham; for much of its length there is the unusual spectacle of three forms of transport cheek by jowl — the Grand Union Canal, the railway and the M1 motorway, an interesting comparison in two centuries of transport development. Earthworks are few on this length apart from the short Stowe Hill Tunnel — well they might be, as a mile beyond Welton, nemesis struck Robert Stephenson and nearly the London & Birmingham as well. In his quest for a straight and level line

Stephenson decided to tunnel under a sandstone ridge at Kilsby.

Three tunnels in British railway history have left their mark as being excessively nasty both in construction and operating discomfort. Blea Moor on the S&C, Woodhead on the Manchester & Sheffield, and Kilsby. A decade later the L&B would have gone up and over the Kilsby Ridge; certainly if Locke had had anything to do with it, as Woodhead put him off tunnels for the rest of his days. The snag with the Kilsby Tunnel was not so much its length, though at $1\frac{1}{4}$ miles it is the longest on the WCML, but that the Kilsby Ridge was not all it seemed to be at first glance. Though like most of the landforms in the south Midlands it ran roughly south-west — north-east it also ran through a hitherto unsuspected geological fault resulting in the tunnellers striking a seam of water bearing quick-sand which drowned out the workings on at least three occasions and all but led to its abandonment and the search for an alternative route. I have been though Kilsby once in the cab of a steam engine and subsequently in the cab of electrics and it is not hard to imagine what conditions must have been like during its construction. Work was undertaken on several faces simultaneously by means of shafts sunk vertically to the working levels and these shafts survive to this day for ventilation. In steam days they did not appear to have much effect on the ventilation as the tunnel was always a 'smokey hole'. My first trip through on an electric loco was an eye opener for every so often there was this mysterious pool of light penetrating into the depths from one of these ventilation shafts. To say the effect was eerie is an understatement.

Once clear of Kilsby the rest of the line to Birmingham was relatively easy from an engineering point of view serving Rugby, then a town of relatively little importance but which blossomed with the coming of the railways, and Coventry in 1837 better known for the antics of Lady Godiva than the manufacture of motor cars. It is an interesting speculation that if Lady G. was on the Board of some of the motor manufacturing firms; would there maybe be a few more cars produced! The final approaches to Birmingham were through a landscape featureless and even being scarred by the Industrial Revolution before the coming of the railway. The original Curzon Street terminus was a Euston in miniature, all facade and no fact. It is still in use as a goods depot today but in greatly altered form. The present Birmingham New Street station is now the nodal point for much of the LMR, serving as it does not only lines from London to the north but the ex-Midland lines from Derby to Bristol. It is an architectural abomination, no doubt on some modern trendy theory that the more important a station is, the uglier it has to be. New Street has the dubious distinction shared with Edinburgh's Waverley of being approached by tunnels in every direction. I can't claim to have known it well in steam days but imagine being set down in a cutting and in a rather confined space it must have been smokey hollow with a vengeance, though strange to say, the photos I have seen taken there in the steam age don't give this impression. I do however remember changing trains there one foggy evening when the atmosphere was opaque to say the least. The modern New Street has been made even more claustrophobic by having a shopping complex built on top of it. In fairness

however having entered from street level you only have to go down to the platforms and they do have escalators... unlike the mountaineering efforts required at Euston which has no escalators other than to the underground. This then is a thumb nail sketch of the London & Birmingham the second (after the Grand Junction) of the main constituents of what was to become the LNW to be completed and still probably the most important. It seems a very far cry from three or four trains a day between the two cities hauled by under-boilered and ill braked locomotives of Mr Bury's and even more antediluvian designs, to the half hourly 100mph electric hauled trains of today. Yet the extraordinary thing is that while certain structures such as bridges and station platforms had to be altered the track alignment was hardly touched. The viaducts and tunnels stand today almost as they were built. There is no doubt that the early railway engineers built to last... in marked contrast to modern road builders, some of whose five-year old concrete elevated roads are already crumbling to ruin.

Below: The inner approaches to many London termini have several 'forgotten' stations that time seems to have passed by and would probably have been closed if anyone remembered they were there! One such was Kilburn High Road the setting in August 1960 for an evening London-Bletchley train hauled rather surprisingly by rebuilt 'Royal Scot' No 46120 *Royal Inniskilling Fusilier.*

Top left: The same August evening in 1960 finds Class 5 No 44940 piloting rebuilt 'Scot' No 46127 *Old Contemptibles* on an early evening express from London-Manchester. This train was regularly double-headed right until the end of steam, by which time the train engine was often one of Longsight's 'Britannias'.

Centre left: Rebuilt 'Scot' No 46158 *The Loyal Regiment* passing South Kenton in August 1950 with a down Manchester express of 15 total. In those days both the Manchester and Liverpool expresses often loaded to 15 or 16 total and the rebuilt 'Scots' appeared to handle them with ease.

Bottom: South Kenton in late 1950 with a Liverpool-London express behind un-rebuilt 'Scot' No 46155 *The Lancer* at a time when the un-rebuilt variety were getting thin on the ground. This to my regret, as I found them very impressive looking and sounding machines.

Top right: Two studies of 'Patriots' at South Kenton in the late summer of 1950. Un-rebuilt 'Patriot' No 45543 *Home Guard* on a heavy down parcels train in black livery with lining on the cab and tender and lettered British Railways.

Centre right: No 45522 *Prestatyn* not long after rebuilding in green livery. This was at the stage when BR were experimenting with various liveries, and if my memory serves me correctly the loco was finished in a lighter shade of green than became standard. An interesting feature of this is that the engine has no smoke deflectors though at this time they were being fitted to the rebuilt 'Scots' as they went through the shops. The train would appear to be composed of steel strips.

Bottom right: A London-Tring evening suburban train passing South Kenton station in June 1960 with Standard 2-6-4T No 80068 The use of big tank engines on the outer suburban services from Euston has a long history from LNW 4-6-2Ts through the Fowler and Stanier 2-6-4T varieties. They also developed a tradition for very fast running between Willesden and Watford, ably maintained by the Standard tanks till the end of steam.

Above: One of the class of engines that will go down in British Railways history as an all time great. Standard 2-10-0 No 92102, not long built at Crewe Works, passes under the GC/Metropolitan Joint line on the southern approach to Kenton with a down train of hopper wagons.

Below: The spacious layout of Kenton station forms the background for this June 1960 shot of the up morning 'Caledonian' nearing the end of its run with an immaculate No 46225 *Duchess of Gloucester* in charge. The LMR/Met electrified line is prominent in the foreground and the relatively spacious goods yard in the background a rather surprising reminder of the railways of two decades ago.

Top right: The Derby designed 4F 0-6-0s were never very popular with the ex-LNW men and their appearance in the London area on the WCML was not all that common. Kenton again forms the background for No 44182 trundling southwards with a lengthy freight in June 1960.

Centre right: In my introduction to this section I mentioned how quickly the London and Birmingham line ran into rural scenery once clear of Willesden. This photo taken between Kenton and Harrow could be 110 miles from Euston not a mere 11. The train from Northampton to London is hauled by one of the Southern designed and Ashford built diesel-electrics No 10203 which during the early 1960s were allocated to the LMR

for diesel evaluation purposes, and worked on anything from the 'Royal Scot' downwards.

Bottom right: The LNW 0-8-0s were very long lived and highly successful machines, known to the men as the 'Super Ds' on account of their being superheated versions of earlier 0-8-0s dating back to the Webb era. They were slow but strong as can be seen in this photograph of No 49441 trundling a heavy freight southwards in rolling country near Headstone Lane in the early summer of 1960.

Left: 'The Lizzies' as the 'Princess Royal' class Pacifics were affectionately referred to by their crews were probably associated with the 'Merseyside Express' more than any other train. In June 1959 No 46203 *Princess Margaret Rose* rolls the up 'Merseyside Express' through the rural parkland north of Headstone Lane while a Euston bound electric lurks in the shadows west of the line.

Below: A relief to the down 'Midday Scot' passes Headstone Lane goods yard in the summer of 1959 with Class 5s Nos 45317 and 45184 in charge. It was one of the odd quirks of loco rostering at the time, that this heavy relief on Saturdays was very often worked by two Class 5s as far as Crewe where a Pacific that had worked south that morning took over.

Top right: Bushey Troughs in July 1960 as 5XP No 45552 *Silver Jubilee* drinks well but not too wisely with a down Birmingham express. This engine was originally LMS No 5642 but was renamed and renumbered in honour of King George V's jubilee in 1935 and adorned in a special black livery with raised chrome boiler bands which which are just discernible under the grime in this photograph.

Bottom right: Approaching Watford Tunnel on the slow lines 5XP No 45586 *Mysore* heads a Bletchley-London local in the late summer of 1960. Rather surprisingly the loco is still paired with the small 'Midland' type tender, for by this time most of the English based 'Jubilees' had high sided Stanier pattern ones, though some of Scotland's allocation went to the scrapyard still with the original low tender.

Above: The first production express type diesel-electrics were the English Electric D200s, subsequently Class 40. Based very much on Ivatt's LMS 'Twins' they were reasonably successful from the start and over the years must have proved a good investment for BR. By present day standards they are heavy and slow, if strong, on the hills. In 1959 and 1960 the outer suburban trains from Euston were often used as running in and driver training duties. In this case a London-Rugby train takes the slow lines between Hemel Hempstead and Berkhamsted with a down stopping train to Rugby with D210 in charge. It is interesting that while this loco was ultimately named *Empress of Britain* in this July 1959 shot it is too new to carry any nameplates.

Left: By some strange freak of all the stations on the old London & Birmingham the only one to have retained the genuine LNW buildings is Berkhamsted, albeit with a modern all-purpose, all hideous synthetic canopy replacing the original one. Some typical LNW station architecture is visible in this photo of a Bletchley-London emu at Berkhamsted on a particularly wet Saturday in the particularly wet summer of 1978.

Above: No 87.032 *Kenilworth* accelerates through Berhamsted after a severe permanent way restriction on 12 August 1978 with the down 'Royal Scot'. There is a slight irony that the prestige train of the West Coast companies should be hauled by a locomotive named after a North British 4-4-0.

Right: The Northchurch Tunnel a mile north of Berkhamsted is a good example of the use of two single bores for the slow lines. As Robert Stephenson found at Watford and more dramatically at Kilsby many of the ridges crossing the path of the London & Birmingham line contained seams of quicksand, and when the line was quadrupled to Roade some of the tunnels were built as single bores to alleviate this trouble. 5XP No 45587 *Baroda* erupts from the Northchurch Tunnel on the down fast line with a Saturday relief to Liverpool in June 1959.

Left: Class 5 No 45101 emerging from the single bore, down slow line, tunnel at Northchurch with a London-Bletchley stopping train in 1960. The engine still having the early type Stanier boiler with the combined dome and top feed which by this time was not common south of the border, but beloved by St Rollox who were 'aye a law unto themselves'.

Below: The enigma. Standard Pacific No 71000 *Duke of Gloucester* a paper rebuild of the ill fated *Princess Anne* (née *Turbomotive*). This three-cylinder Caprotti valvegeared Pacific is seen here at Northchurch in July 1959 on the down 'Midday Scot' which was probably the highspot of her undistinguished career. Thrown in with the Crewe North Pacific link she was never liked, being considered very heavy on coal; when compared with the *Duchess of Gloucester* the distaff side won hands down.

Right: In the typical rolling wooded country of the Chilterns between Berkhamsted and Tring 'Patriot' No 45518 *Bradshaw* coasts Londonwards with an express from Liverpool in 1959. The 'Patriots' seemed to thrive on heavy trains and right to the end of their days were frequently used on heavy loaded Saturday extras such as this.

Below: Between Weedon and Welton the Grand Union Canal, the LNW main line and the M1 motorway all run cheek by jowl. On 8 June 1960 5XP No 45733 *Novelty* skirts the newly opened M1 near Welton with an up Saturday relief from Liverpool to London. The line of the canal is just visible behind the trees in the background.

Top left: The Stanier Moguls tended to be most elusive engines, at least in my experience. However, on Saturday 8 June 1960 No 42953 heads southwards with a long parcels train near Welton. It is hard to realise that these engines for all their small appearance and 2-6-0 wheel arrangement were in the Class 5 power category. The sign between train and the edge of the motorway indicates the proximity of the now notorious Watford Gap service station.

Centre left: Rebuilt 'Patriot' No 45534 *E. Tootal Broadhurst* near Welton with a down Manchester Express, loaded on this summer Saturday to 15 total. Such loads the rebuilt 'Scots' and 'Patriots' appeared to handle with ease even if the schedules were slow by modern standards. The lack of traffic on the motorway compared with today has a certain aura of a Hitchcock film . . . but at this time in 1960 the M1 was considered something for motorists to be very wary of.

Bottom left: No 46229 *Duchess of Hamilton* running hard between Weedon and Welton with the down 'Midday Scot' on Saturday 8 June 1960. This engine after a sojourn at Butlins Camp at Minehead is now in the National Railway Museum at York and it is hoped to restore her to working order.

Top right: Until the coming of the London & Birmingham, Rugby was a small if prosperous market town serving a rich agricultural area. The London & Birmingham and Trent Valley lines plus several other minor branches altered all that and it became a railway centre of some importance drawing industry in its wake. Class 87 electric No 87.023 named *Highland Chieftain* the week after this photo was taken on 20 May 1978 approaches Rugby from the north with an up Blackpool express. *David M. Cross*

Centre right: A special train from Congleton to Euston approaching Rugby made up of three AM10 emu sets in May 1978. The use of emus for relatively long distance journeys over the electrified section of the WCML line south of Crewe and Birmingham has been one of the more surprising features of electrification, as I can imagine more comfortable vehicles for journeys of over 100 miles. *David M. Cross*

Bottom right: One of the main industries attracted to Rugby by its excellent rail communications both from the LNW, and latterly the London extension of the Great Central (now closed), was the electrical industry notably the companies that merged to form GEC whose factory dominates the background in this photograph. Diesel-electric No 25.111 waits while doing some dilatory shunting as No 86.018 sweeps into the station with a special from Preston to London. *David M. Cross*

Above: One of the most dramatic features of the West Coast electrification has been the elimination of most signal boxes and the concentration of the control of miles of track in one box. This has been taken to its limit between Crewe and Glasgow, but even in the early stages south of Crewe a great deal of signalling was centralised in electronic wonderlands: such as Rugby power box seen as a background to No 86.023 with the Kensington-Perth Motorail on 20 May 1978. *David M. Cross*

Left: It is to be hoped that 'Lady Godiva' had more elegant lines than this Class 31, No 31.232 seen entering Coventry station in May 1978 with the 06.30 Paddington-Birmingham train via Oxford. The use of 31s on these trains is not common, their hauling being normally in the hands of Class 47s or 50s. *David M. Cross*

Above right: A more normal scene at Coventry in May 1978 as an AM4 electric multiple-unit waits in the platform with a Birmingham-Rugby stopping train while No 86.007 coasts past light engine. *David M. Cross*

Right: A pastoral idyll within 10 miles of the centre of Birmingham. No E3111 (now No 86.024) crossing a stream near Hampton-in-Arden with the 14.40 Euston-Wolverhampton express. The setting is so unexpected in the 'Black Country' that it could well be mistaken for Westmorland. Still at one stage in early railway history Hampton-in-Arden assumed considerable importance as a junction with a line from Burton-on-Trent that figured largely in the ferocious infighting among the rival companies that finally formed the Midland. *David M. Cross*

Left: Class 87s at Birmingham New Street. No 87.033 subsequently named *Thane of Fife* waits to leave with the 14.05 express to Glasgow while sister engine No 87.005, now *City of London,* as yet un-named has arrived with a London-Birmingham express on 20 May 1978. The cause of the current claustrophobia at New Street is well shown by the garish sign above No 87.005. *David M. Cross*

Below left: Whatever may be said for or against Birmingham New Street today it cannot be faulted for variety of modern motive power. This photo taken on 6 May 1978 has a good selection at the east end of the station. No 47.122 waits to leave with an express to Paddington via Oxford. Class 87 No 87.029 *Earl Marischal* is arriving with a Wolverhampton-Euston express, while in the middle an AM10 electric multiple-unit waits to follow with a stopping train to Euston.

Right: Birmingham New Street quite apart from being set in the bowels of the earth is approached by tunnels in every direction. In this 1978 photo No 86.211 approaches from the west end of the station with a through train from Liverpool to Southampton.

Below: Notwithstanding the traffic from the LNW lines, New Street handles a considerable amount of trains on the NE-SW route as shown in this photo of No 45.027 emerging into the station from the murk of one of the tunnels at the west end with an Exeter-Manchester train on what was formerly the Midland line from Bristol to Derby and the north-east.

The Grand Junction and Ramifications

This title covers the area of south Lancashire, Staffordshire and parts of Cheshire where the railway pattern has been influenced by the building of the Grand Junction line between Newton Junction ($4\frac{1}{2}$ miles north of Warrington) on the Liverpool & Manchester line and Birmingham. It was opened in July 1837 thus beating the London & Birmingham to the latter place by nearly a year, though in fairness the L&B was badly delayed by the notorious Kilsby Tunnel. To fully appreciate the building and layout of the Grand Junction it is necessary to go back to the dawn of main line railway history, the Liverpool and Manchester. This line opened between the two cities in 1830 was surveyed and engineered by George Stephenson and was typical of his, and later his son Robert's work, in so far as they would go straight if possible even if it meant tunnels and the crossing of the notorious Chat Moss. In both these cases Locke; who was working for the elder Stephenson at the time had a big hand, in the case of Chat Moss amicably, though he said afterwards that he would never have contemplated the Moss but would have gone round it. The tunnel episodes were not as happy, as Locke found that some of George Stephensons surveys in the Liverpool area were wildly wrong and this started a friction between the two men that was to boil over when the Grand Junction came to be built. Apart from the great cuttings and tunnelling on the approaches to Liverpool, the Liverpool & Manchester was a featureless and flat line. In the early days of railways mention is made frequently of 'The Liverpool Party'. These were a group of far-sighted, wealthy Liverpool merchants for in the 1830s Liverpool was a place of considerable importance based mainly on trade from abroad. These men realised that if Liverpool's shipping facilities could be connected to Birmingham's industrial ones, it would be a considerable boon to both places. The projection of a line from London to Birmingham stimulated this and so the idea of the Grand Junction was born.

The country between them was not difficult, the two main barriers being the valleys of the River Mersey and Weaver and one or two other smaller rivers in the Wolverhampton-Birmingham area. The line was to be built under the aegis of George Stephenson with Locke as his assistant and intially Stephenson, though in overall command, took charge of the Whitmore-Birmingham section while Locke was left with the detailed planning of the northern and more difficult portion. It soon became apparent that the approach to their respective sections was very different, with Locke's meticulous estimates and insistance that his contractors adhered to them, in marked contrast with Stephensons somewhat inaccurate estimates and slapdash contracting. Tension mounted and in the end Locke was made responsible for the whole line by the influential Liverpool promoters with the result that the oft exaggerated feud between Stephenson (Snr) and Locke came into being. Before describing the line in more detail mention must be made of the $4\frac{1}{4}$-mile Warrington & Newton Junction Railway which had been built by local enterprise to link Warrington with the Liverpool and Manchester. The promoters of the Grand Junction tacitly assumed that they would get this for a song, but the good citizens of Warrington had other ideas and a mighty row developed. Everyone tried to play off everyone else: the lawyers as usual waxed fat. In the end only the threat of a completely new line by way of the Runcorn Gap brought the little Warrington & Newton Company to its senses. The line through Runcorn was ultimately built with its magnificent bridge over the Mersey and is today the main line from Liverpool to the south.

There were no features of note on the line between Warrington and Newton Junction apart from a very cramped and inconvenient layout at the latter. However immediately south of

Warrington came the first major engineering work on the line, the viaduct over the Mersey. This viaduct while still in use has been superseded on the West Coast main line of today by a higher and more dramatic structure to the west. Then five miles to the south came the viaduct over the Weaver Valley at Dutton, an even more impressive structure still used by the main line to the north. Hence southward to the then very rural village of Coppenhall, subsequently to become the great railway town of Crewe, the land was flat and the construction easy. It is south of Crewe that we get the first sight of Locke's advanced thinking in the matter of steam locomotive power. Up until that time the idea of any lengthy grade of more than about 1 in 300 was out of the question but Locke foresaw quicker than anyone else that the steam engine was bound to become a more powerful machine than the Liverpool & Manchester variety and various effete efforts of Mr Bury and others. South of Crewe lay one of the transverse ridges that had given Robert Stephenson so much trouble on the London & Birmingham and Locke made his line climb over this for about nine miles to a summit at Whitmore on grades as steep in places as 1 in 177. This caused consternation among engineers of the day, though 10 years later things had changed to such an extent that 10 miles averaging 1 in 70 over Beattock had become a practicable proposition. One wonders with hindsight that if Robert Stephenson had shared Lockes confidence in the increasing power of the steam locomotive, whether the London & Birmingham and that dreadful Kilsby Tunnel would have been built as they were. Madeley Bank as this incline between Crewe and Whitmore came to be known is a beautifully engineered stretch of line with its sweeping curves and views for miles in either direction across the gently rolling wooded Cheshire landscape. Even in the days of big Pacifics it was no sinecure, and several firemen from Crewe have told me they would sooner tackle Shap with an engine well warmed up, than Madeley with one staring 'cold' from Crewe. The southern descent from Whitmore to Stafford was more gentle with no grades steeper than 1 in 398, again showing the Locke hallmark of using the landforms where he could rather than cutting through them. The result is a splendid line of gracious sweeping curves.

The story of Stafford is in many ways comparable with that of Rugby, where what had been a small and prosperous market town was transformed into a considerable industrial one by the coming of the railway. Beyond Stafford the line is relatively flat the only feature of note being the Penkridge Viaduct, and it is worth mentioning in passing that it was some wildly inaccurate over estimating on the part of George Stephenson for this structure that was the last straw that broke the Liverpool Parties back, and led to his virtual dismissal as engineer to the Grand Junction. Truth be told old George having been brought up on the short

mineral lines of the north-east lacked the grandeur of vision needed for the coming era of great trunk lines whereas the younger engineers, his son Robert, Locke and Brunel did not have the handicaps of chaldrons of coals hung about their necks. Thanks mainly to Locke's insistance on accurate costings and surveys the Grand Junction progressed rapidly and was built well and relatively cheaply. The approach to Wolverhampton necessitated a short climb of 1 in 101 but as this was only for a mile it did not create the consternation of Madeley. The change south of Wolverhampton is nothing if not dramatic, the rolling shires give way to the blackest of the 'Black Country'. It may well have been scarred even before the line was built but today must rate as the most depressing in all Britain with derelict factories and turgid canals and streams. The structural nature of the line also alters as it changes from long easy grades with great sweeping curves to a series of short and in places sharp ups and downs with many twists and turns. The original Grand Junction shared the Curzon Street station with the London & Birmingham but owing to objections from a local landowner had to make a wide detour to the east. Thanks to the troubles at Kilsby the Grand Junction was opened throughout from Liverpool before the line from Euston, not that this mattered as both terminated at Curzon Street and no through running as such was possible.

So much for the basic Grand Junction Line. Its ramifications became many; not the least important of which was to be the Trent Valley line from Stafford to Rugby by-passing the Birmingham conurbation, and which is now the main line from London to the north. At Stafford it leaves the direct line to Birmingham on a sharp curve to the east which has necessitated speed restrictions right up until the present day. Thereafter it has many of the features of the length from Crewe to Stafford passing in the main though rolling pastoral country broken only by the South Staffordshire coalfield round Rugeley and Atherstone. It is a line that has been remarkably little photographed and I have to confess to having no photos of it at all in this book, which is a pity as there must have been some attractive spots on it. It was triggered initially by nasty noises from Manchester who thought that Liverpool was hogging too much of the communications in the area and made threats about building a line of their own to Birmingham by way of Stoke, much of which was built subsequently as the North Staffordshire, that connected into the Trent Valley at Culwich, as by then it had no option for the Trent Valley had effectively cut it off from a direct route to Birmingham. The Trent Valley line is interesting in that the route was surveyed by Locke but the line ultimately built by Robert Stephenson and shows an interesting blend of the characters of the two men. Fortunately the country it passed through was relatively easy and there were no great complications as to whether it should go up and over or round in the Locke mould, or tunnel and cut through as per Stephenson. The last main part of the Grand Junction complex was the direct line from Liverpool to Weaver Junction north of Crewe by way of the Runcorn Gap, the outstanding engineering feature of which is the great steel bridge at Runcorn, not exactly a thing of beauty but highly impressive none the less.

With the coming of the railway the whole area round Liverpool developed into a highly industrialised complex and railways were spawned in all directions, first by the Grand Junction but then by the LNW following the logical amalgamations of the various west coast companies completed in 1860. While Liverpool may have been the prime mover in the formation of the Grand Junction and all the lines in the area afterwards, the most outstanding chapter in the whole history of the railways in the Birmingham-Liverpool-Manchester triangle undoubtedly must be the meteoric rise in the town of Crewe. In a matter of a very few years the rural fastness of Church Coppenhall was turned into a major railway town. Not only did it have the biggest locomotive works in Britain, and at one time in the world, but it became a junction of the greatest importance. There is no doubt that even in the early surveys of the Grand Junction, Locke had in his mind that Coppenhall (soon to be renamed Crewe after Crewe Hall the seat of the local landowner) would be a possible junction with lines to Chester on one hand and Manchester on the other. In 1840 the Chester & Crewe Railway was completed probably surveyed by Locke though the line passed through

flat country without any major engineering works and so was not a hard proposition. In the same year the Manchester & Birmingham was opened as far as Stockport with the intention of going to Birmingham by way of Stoke. This was dropped when the Grand Junction by means of some very dubious promises not to be fulfilled in the event suggested that it would be better if they built their line to join the Grand Junction at Crewe, which after a lot of duplicity was duly done, though for some years the wretched Manchester Company had its own station literally across the road from the Grand Junction. Still by the early 1840s Crewe was a junction to be reckoned with, subsequent lines to Shrewsbury and Stoke made it all important between London and Carlisle.

Quite apart from its geographical importance as a junction what really made Crewe was the decision that their locomotive works at Edgehill were too cramped for the rapidly increasing traffic and that they should be moved lock, stock and barrel to Crewe. There was plenty of flat land available not only for the works but for a new town that had to be built for the workforce. With the establishment of Crewe Works not only was the company able to maintain its own locomotives but to build them, as previously most engines were bought from outside contractors, a practice that continues in America to this day. Crewe expanded very rapidly both as a junction and especially under Webb as a great railway works. The present passenger station even prior to electrification had been rebuilt twice and a vast complex of avoiding lines for goods traffic laid to the west, which by means of burrowing junctions could connect to any of the

main lines out of Crewe without fouling the passenger ones. A vast marshalling yard was constructed at Basford Hall about a mile to the south of the station and apart from the works there were two large sheds, Crewe North that handled most of the passenger workings and Crewe South for freight traffic. Today with the total electrification of the Anglo/Scottish service Crewe has declined somewhat in importance, especially from a locomotive point of view as engine changing between London and the north is no longer necessary. Even so it is a very busy place and all trains for North Wales change from electric to diesel traction there. I have devoted a lot of space to Crewe as it was the first true railway town, built by the Grand Junction for its own needs and convenience. In a way it could probably claim to be the first 'New Town' in Britain, though I am sure would not want to do so in the light of some postwar monstrosities saddled with this stigma.

In illustrating this section I have more or less set down the barrow and handed over to my son, the result of which is that many of the photos are of modern forms of traction. Not that I find this in anyway a drawback for as I said in my introduction diesels and electrics seem more a part of the industrial scene than steam ever did. Unfortunately neither of us can illustrate the Trent Valley line as we never wandered aimlessly... to quote the dictionary definition of 'roaming', in that area though I did on one occasion nearly cause a major traffic accident near Atherstone by spotting the NCB Garratt in its last days and stopping abruptly in a stream of fairly fast moving traffic on the A5.

Below: Rebuilt 'Scot' No 46110 *Grenadier Guardsman* in Crewe station in September 1960 with a Manchester-Birmingham train. While at this time steam was still king at Crewe the writing was on the wall as the modern signals and electric overheads are already in position.

Top right and centre right: Contrasts at Crewe Works. Class 40 No 40.043 in the process of being cut up on 3 April 1977. The locomotive has been cut in half and all the motors and generators removed. By way of contrast on 18 May 1973 No E3071 (now 85.016) emerges from the electric maintenance depot after an overhaul of its electric equipment. No 86.003 waits alongside for testing and shows the contrast between the smart and eye catching raised chrome numbers of the first batch of electrics and the more prosaic style of today. *David M. Cross*

Bottom right: The last all Pullman train in Britain, the up 'Manchester Pullman' slips through Crewe station on 23 July 1976 with No 86.226 in charge. While lacking much of the interest of steam days there is no doubt that, as this photo shows, the new Crewe is a cleaner brighter place. *David M. Cross*

Above: The rarely seen side of Crewe. Train 6V78 the 17.15 from Northwich to Baglan Bay bulk salt train on the goods lines that avoid Crewe station to the west. The train is approaching Salop Goods Junction on 23 July 1976 with No 47.228 in charge. *David M. Cross*

Left: Salop Goods Junction is again the setting for train 4067 the Aintree-Southampton Freightliner composed mainly of OCL containers for shipment from Southampton. The Crewe goods lines were highly complex and No 47.332 is crossing some intricate pointwork on 23 July 1976. *David M. Cross*

Above right: Owing to the elaborate goods lines avoiding Crewe station to the west it was very rare to see a goods train pass through the passenger station. However for some unknown reason on 22 July 1970 Class 24s Nos D5018 and D5016 ran through the station with a bulk coal train from the south for the Manchester line. In the background Class 40, D233 still named *Empress of England* waits to work an express forward to North Wales.

Right: Undoubtedly one of the most attractive parts of the main line south of Crewe was the Madeley Bank with its sweeping curves and 1 in 177 grades which could make life hard for engines starting cold from Crewe. Rebuilt 'Scot' No 46155 *The Lancer* makes a vigorous attack on the Madeley Bank with an Edinburgh-Birmingham express in September 1960.

Left: The down 'Lake Express' descending the Madeley Bank near Betley Road behind 'Duchess' class Pacific No 46225 *Duchess of Gloucester* on 12 September 1960 shortly before the overhead wires were erected in connection with the London, Liverpool & Manchester electrification. This must have been the spot where sister engine No 6220 *Coronation* attained 114mph on the now notorious press run in 1937.

Below: The Stanier Moguls always seemed to be remarkably sure footed engines, as shown by the lack of effort being made by No 42981 lifting a heavy parcels train on the 1 in 177 between Betley Road and Madeley on a warm September afternoon in 1960. This picture was taken in the months preceding the erection of the electric overhead lines south of Crewe.

Right: The old order at Madeley in 1949. A very grubby rebuilt 'Scot' No 46116 *Irish Guardsman* coasts down the bank with the down 'Lakes Express', the loco is still without the smoke deflectors which while no doubt helping the crews of the rebuilt 'Scots' did nothing to improve their looks. On the up fast line 'Patriot' No 45517 works a fitted freight to Willesden.

Below right: Stafford station on 27 April 1975 when the electric power was switched off between there and Crewe. Train 1A10 the Sunday morning Blackpool-Euston express arrived with Class 50 No 50.008 towing No 86.226 'dead' with its pantograph lowered. Such workings on Sundays over the WCML are not uncommon to allow essential maintenance work on the electric overheads.

Left: Stafford station on 6 July 1974. Class 86/2 No 86.210 pauses with the 11.20 Liverpool-Birmingham train while an electric multiple-unit waits to follow with a stopping train for Nuneaton. *David M. Cross*

Below left: While the new Wolverhampton (High Level) station has the all purpose concrete and glass 'image' of the LMR electrification it is a distinct improvement on the old Grand Junction station which from memory was gloomy in the extreme. Electric multiple-unit No 312204 waits to work a stopping train to Birmingham on 3 April 1976; this was one of a batch of electric units designed on the lines of the Great Northern line ones that have been constructed for working shuttle trains between Birmingham New Street and Birmingham International. *David M. Cross*

Right: The line between Wolverhampton and Birmingham defies all efforts to be photogenic but this photo of Class 47 No 1595 passing through Coseley Deepfields on 15 December 1972 gives some idea of the blackest parts of the 'Black Country'. The train is a BSC company train of metal bars from Bilston to Toton and is of interest in that it is equipped not with one, but two, brake tenders behind the locomotive. *David M. Cross*

Below: This photo may not have launched a 1,000 ships but it nearly wrote off 100 motor cars. Driving north on the A5 in May 1960 just north of Atherstone this vision appeared, if not out of the blue at least out of the bushes, and without thinking I stopped . . . abruptly, an act not appreciated by my fellow motorists or sundry lorry drivers. The last Garratt to work in Britain, NCB's *William Francis* marshalling a train of empty wagons at the interchange sidings between the NCB and BR at Atherstone. It must be one of the last photos taken of this engine in action as it was retired soon afterwards and the nearest I have of any photos on the Trent Valley line!

Left: Liverpool Lime Street in the modern era. The station clean and light without the smoking of steam engines. A Trans-Pennine dmu from Hull has just arrived while a suburban unit waits to depart, with a line of locos waiting their next turn in the centre road. The contrast between this photo and some of Eric Treacys' early work in the sulphurous caverns before the war is remarkable, but nobody nowadays with all lines signalled in both directions, would venture into the caverns beyond the end of the platform. *David M. Cross*

Below left: One of the great advantages of electric power is that locomotives between trips do not need to go to sheds for servicing and can be parked in the handiest place for their next turns of duty. This is well illustrated by this photo of Liverpool's Lime Street in July 1973 with a line of electric locomotives parked in the centre road between platforms 3 and 4 waiting their next turns of duty. Nos E3162, E3188 and 86.005 are the electrics in question. *David M. Cross*

Above: 1F19 a Sunday London-Liverpool express enters Runcorn station on a day when the electric power was cut off for maintenance on the overheads. On such occasions the diesel power was normally provided as far as Crewe by one of the latter's numerous Class 47s. However on 12 August 1973 Class 50 No 419 found itself deputising for an electric. *David M. Cross*

Right: Runcorn station was the junction for a short branch to Runcorn Docks on the Manchester Ship Canal. In this photo in August 1973 Class 40 No D212 (formerly *Aureol*) comes off the Runcorn Dock branch with a permanent way special from Folly Lane, passing sister engine No D330 parked in a siding. The lines on the right of the picture are the main Liverpool-Weaver Junction ones via the Runcorn bridge. *David M. Cross*

Above: Possibly the best known name in British railway history, Rainhill, scene of the famous locomotive trials prior to the inauguration of the Liverpool & Manchester Railway in 1830. The station is still in use today and the site of the trials commemorated by a plaque on the platform. *David M. Cross*

Left: Train 1A69 the 17.04 Liverpool-London passing Allerton station on the outskirts of Liverpool hauled by Nos 50.040 and 87.015. The date was 8 August 1975 shortly after the Weaver Junction smash had lead to all sorts of diversions in the Liverpool/Crewe area. The interesting point about this photograph is that most unusually for a diesel plus electric combination; the electric has the pantograph raised and is presumably working. *David M. Cross*

Above right: Another photo at Allerton on 8 August 1975 following the Weaver Junction accident. The 11.50 London-Liverpool express hauled by No 40.073 diverted by way of Frodsham Junction and Chester. *David M. Cross*

Right: Class 25 No 25.242 pulls out of Prescot with a short freight for Garston on 13 April 1977. The train is leaving the BICC sidings, and in the background are some of the 70ft German ferry wagons that are used to take cables direct from Prescot to Harwich then by ferry to Hook of Holland, from whence they are distributed direct all over Europe.

Left: A Liverpool-Hull Trans-Pennine dmu passes through Huyton station on the original Liverpool & Manchester line in March 1977. *David M. Cross*

Centre left: A Blackpool-London express pauses in Warrington (Bank Quay) on 1 June 1973. The loco is Class 50 numbered at that time 428 without the 'D' prefix and, before the introduction of five figure numbers. It was the four miles from Warrington to Newton Junction that proved to be a bone of considerable contention in the early days of the Grand Junction line. In the background an elderly Park Royal dmu waits with a train from Manchester to North Wales. *David M. Cross*

Bottom left: The complications of Newton Junction could not last as north/south traffic on the WCML began to build up so a spur was built passing under the Liverpool & Manchester line to join what had been built as the Wigan & Newton Railway from Parkside Junction on the L&M to Wigan Wallgate. This spur is now a part of the West Coast main line and diverged from the original Grand Junction at Winwick Junction. No 86.249 approaches Winwick with the 15.00 London-Carlisle in June 1977. The turnout at Winwick is relatively sharp necessitating a speed restriction even today. *David M. Cross*

Top right: A northbound oil train from Stanlow (Shell) Sidings, reporting number 6F55 approaching Winwick Junction on 9 June 1977. Class 47, No 47.197 towing a failed Class 40 No 40.035. *David M. Cross*

Centre right: Strictly speaking the Wigan area has nothing to do with the Grand Junction as it was built as the Wigan & Newton Railway and remained as such until amalgamation with the North Union, and then finally absorbed by the LNW. Still, geographical considerations make me include Wigan with the other lines in this section. Class 40 No 40.191 pauses at Springs Branch (Wigan) with a Bold Colliery to Bickershaw Colliery empty mgr set in March 1977. *David M. Cross*

Bottom right: HST set No 253.022 between Springs Branch and Wigan on a test run between Penrith and Crewe with the reporting number IT23, on 13 April 1977. These regular paths for testing of both diesel and electric power are an interesting feature of WCML operation, over the past two decades providing a great variety of power from GT3 to HST. *David M. Cross*

Left and centre left: Class 87 No 87.016 subsequently named *Sir Francis Drake* passing Springs Branch (Wigan) on 20 May 1977 with the ECS of the new Royal Train en route from Mossend Yard (Glasgow) to Wolverhampton. This was one of the many Royal Train workings in connection with 1977 jubilee tours and like all Royal Trains ECS has the reporting number 1X00. It is of interest that even empty Royal Trains run as Class 1 workings, where as most empty stock trains are in the Class 3 category. *David M. Cross*

Below: By way of contrast the old Royal Train near Wigan Canal in May 1977 with Class 40s in charge. Nos 40.025 and 40.109 head southwards with the 10.45 empty royal stock from Barrow to Furness-to-Wolverton. This is possibly one of the last occasions that the old Royal Train was used, and the use of Class 40s was necessary as this set was not equipped for electric train heating. *David M. Cross*

Above right: The motive power depot at Wigan had the delightful name of Springs Branch . . . more suited I would have thought to the Scottish Highlands than Industrial Lancashire, but the name originated from a line built around 1835 to serve one of the collieries that were the raison d'etre for the Wigan & Hewton Railway. An open day at Springs Branch depot on 7 July 1973 finds a Class 40 No 218 *Carmenia* with the breakdown crane and Class 25 No 5260 on display. *David M. Cross*

Below right: Wigan Wallgate on 19 September 1975 with Class 50 No 50.040 on 1M29 the Sunday morning Glasgow-Liverpool express, which had been diverted by the old L&Y line from Lostock Junction; after a reversal there having come from Preston by way of Chorley. This rather attractive rural tour of south Lancashire was quite common at the time while major engineering works were being undertaken between Boars Head and Standish. *David M. Cross*

Welsh Incursions

The ventures into Wales of the old London & North Western fall into four categories. The most important and in many ways the most straightforward being the great main line along the North Wales coast and across Angelsey to the port of Holyhead. The other main line was from Shrewsbury to Hereford which was joint with the GWR and at the time was a case of fortune making very strange bedfellows, though in the case of the Shrewsbury & Hereford things seemed to run amicably enough. The third and in many ways the most interesting, certainly the most scenic was the Central Wales line that ran from the Shrewsbury & Hereford at Craven Arms to Swansea and Carmarthen. In this case, the GWR, once again owned part of the right of way south of Llandilo. The final of the LNW's Welsh incursions was 'the Head of the Valleys' line from Abergavenny Junction to Merthyr with various branches reaching down into the weathly mining valleys of South Wales. This isolated outpost of the LNW I fear cannot be illustrated which is a pity as it must have had some highly spectacular lengths, it certainly had some ferocious grades. I never even saw these lines let alone photographed them, and one of the strange things is that few other people appear to have either. Though the 'Head of the Valleys' line was completely isolated from the rest of the LNW system, it was at one time a highly important link in getting South Wales coal to the industrial Midlands and north. The link with the north being made over pure GWR lines between Abergavenny and Hereford thence over the Shrewsbury & Hereford Joint line and then by pure LNW metals to Crewe. These Welsh mineral lines have now all been closed. The Central Wales line remains open but a pale shadow of its former self, as the once heavy coal traffic from the Swansea area to the north is now routed by Cardiff, but has declined greatly in the past few years. Still thanks to some very spirited opposition from the local population the Central Wales has survived with an adequate, if none too frequent, passenger service and is becoming increasingly important for excursion traffic. The latter being an interesting throwback to its early days when various Wells in Radnorshire, whose names all began with Ll and were totally unpronouncable, enjoyed a great reputation as health resorts for Victorian hypochondriacs.

However the most important of the LNW's Welsh incursions was undoubtedly the Chester & Holyhead route, known for a long time as the Royal Mail route on account of the importance of the Irish mail traffic up until World War I. It is a line of intense contrasts and great bridges, indeed the final 40 miles from Llandudno Junction to Holyhead must be among the most interesting lengths of main line railway in Britain. Robert Stephenson was the engineer from Chester westwards, the Crewe & Chester Railway having been built some years previously under the general guidance of Locke, but probably by Locke's new protege Errington. Immediately west of Chester comes a short tunnel through stable sedimentary rock, then the River Dee is crossed near Saltney Junction on an elaborate steel girder bridge carrying four tracks, two of which diverge to the south to form the ex-GWR Shrewsbury and Chester lines. It was the fall of this bridge in 1847 when a Chester-Ruabon train was passing over it that nearly ruined Robert Stephenson's career and set the Chester & Holyhead back on its heels. While Stephenson was exonerated from blame at the enquiry, the whole principle of the use of long cast iron girders on railway bridges fell into disrepute. This was to have a dramatic effect on the other great bridges on the line at Conway and Menai Straits. Between Saltney Junction and Llandudno the railway followed the coast on relatively level and stable ground with no notable features from either a geological or engineering point of view. What was of interest however was the social implications of a railway to this part of the coast, handy as it was to the rapidly growing industrial conurbations of Liverpool, Manchester and to a lesser extent Birmingham. With the coming of the railway 'a day by the sea' became a possibility for the people in these cities, a fact that the Chester & Holyhead were not slow to realise, as was the LNW when the two companies amalgamated. The result of this was an explosive development of the North Wales coast as a tourist area and the rise of towns such as Rhyl, Prestatyn, Colwyn Bay and Llandudno. Indeed so great did the tourist traffic become that much of the line was quadrupled under the aegis of the LNW, though the extra tracks have been lifted in most parts in recent years as the railways lost out to the motor-car for holiday travel.

If the line east of Llandudno Junction had been level and relatively easy to build the next 40 miles most certainly were not. In the family tradition Robert Stephenson built on the 'straight through' theory, but in view of the nature of the landforms it is hard to see how he could have done anything else. Immediately west of Llandudno Junction the tidal estuary of the River Conway had to be bridged. To make matters worse immediately west of the crossing the walls of Conway Castle had to be skirted and then the old town wall cut through. With the memory of the collapse of the Dee bridge at Chester fresh in his mind Stephenson took no chances and the railway ran in twin tubular steel 'tunnels' supported on stone pillars. At the west end of this unique structure (at the time) every effort was made to make the bridge/tunnel entrances harmonise with the adjoining castle; and the old town walls likewise were raised to form a bridge over the line still in keeping with their original character. Recently a school of thought has come to criticise these embellishments as bogus and in bad taste. Personally I couldn't disagree more. Considering that the station was built in the old town nearly under the wall and a small goods yard sandwiched between the castle walls and the running line I find that Stephenson and his architects did a superbly good job of harmonising the railway with its surroundings . . . one shudders to think what modern engineers of the concrete and plastic school would have done. Fortunately it wouldn't have lasted nearly as long as the present Conway Bridge. Beyond Conway the line followed yet another strip of sandy coast but with the hills crowding in on the landward side with two short tunnels through spurs of hard slates at Penmaenbach and Penmaenmawr Head. Beyond this the country tends to open out again but the hills are never far away. It is of interest that it was between Penmaenmawr and Bangor that Ramsbottom laid the first set of watertroughs in the world near the small village of Aber. These were laid down to enable the small engines of the time to tackle the 84 miles between Holyhead and Chester non-stop, an unheard of feat at the time. The reason for this was not for the benefit of the passengers, but for the benefit of the Post Office who at that time considered they had the un-alienable right to dictate to even such a lordly company as the LNW, though in fairness to the PO the Irish Mails were of considerable importance and they did give a good service for one penny in marked contrast to today's appalling performance for nine confetti pence.

The only town of importance between Llandudno and Holyhead was Bangor which retained a great deal of LNW flavour until very recently and was approached by short tunnels through the slates at either end but lacked the claustrophobia of New Street. A mile and a half beyond Bangor came the highlight of the whole line, Stephenson's magnificent tubular bridge across the Menai Strait. It is a happy event in railway history that the three great second generation railway engineers, Brunel, Locke and Robert Stephenson himself were all present when the last girder was hoisted into position. A less happy chapter in the history of this remarkable structure occurred in the early 1970s when vandals set fire to one of the tubes causing such damage that the bridge had to be closed for six months and is now considerably altered in appearance as a result of repairs and partial rebuilding. The route across Anglesey while devoid of any marked geological features is very different from the typical Stephenson line in having many short sharp gradients though still holding to his principle that the shortest distance between two points is a straight line, even if it entailed having a station with the longest name in Britain which I can neither spell nor pronounce. Holyhead Harbour on its exposed islet has been subject to many alterations in its history and is without the scope of

this book, other that the interesting fact that one of the smallest class of BR diesel shunters work continuously on the outer breakwater... there were originally two of the 01 class but now there is only one being kept going by faith and spare parts from the withdrawn one.

In the hey-day of the LNW and well into LMS times the Chester & Holyhead line boasted several branches to places in the hills as Bethesda, Llanberis and one that survives to this day from Llandudno to Blaenau Festiniog. Another ran from Menai Bridge Junction to Carnarvon and an extraordinary link with the Cambrian Coast line in the middle of nowhere at a place with the improbable name of Afon Wen... this last being the LNW's last approach to west Wales and having seen Afon Wen I find it easy to see why they went no further.

The other main line under the category of Welsh incursions hardly touched Wales at all but ran through the beautiful border country from Shrewsbury to Hereford. This line was a joint LNW/GWR venture built originally under the auspices of Thomas Brassey. It

is a very beautiful line running under the shadows of the Long Mynd and Wenlock Edge. It was linked with the LNW by the Shrewsbury & Crewe which running across the South Cheshire and north Shropshire plains posed neither great earthworks nor difficult gradients. Indeed the Crewe-Shrewsbury line seems to have appeared on the Victorian railway scene almost un-noticed. The GWR connected with this line at Shrewsbury in the north with a line from Wolverhampton to Chester and at the south end with lines from Hereford to Newport and Hereford to Worcester. Considering that the LNW and GWR and their forebears fought so bitterly over Shrewsbury it is surprising that the Shrewsbury & Hereford enjoyed such a placid and indeed prosperous existence for so long. Perhaps the delightful nature of the country it passed through, and charming old towns such as Ludlow had something to do with its rustic tranquility. There is even a story told of this line that at one time the booking office and waiting rooms at Moreton-on-Lugg were in the hollow stem of an ancient oak tree. No doubt this sylvan idyll soon succumbed to the fire throwing antics of some of the LNW locomotives. While scenically most attractive this line boasted few major engineering features, but had a long stiff climb from Shrewsbury to Church Stretton summit, in places as steep as 1 in 90. There is an interesting story about this line, in that the LNW banned the GWR using 4-6-0 locomotives on it for a long time, officially on the grounds of weight but probably as they had none of their own. Luckily it is one of the lines now permitted for steam operation, and there could hardly be a better choice as it is a very lovely line.

At Craven Arms some 20 miles south of Shrewsbury the LNW threw off its final incursion into Wales and this was the most fascinating of them all, the Central Wales. This was no placid English railway, both structurally and scenically it owed much to the Highlands of Scotland, but unlike the lines of the Highlands for many years it carried a very heavy freight traffic between the northern industrial areas and the Swansea area; also at one time a multitude of through coaches from the north and even from Euston which got to Swansea slightly quicker than the GWR before the completion of the Severn Tunnel, which must have galled the latter greatly. Bearing sharply westwards at Craven Arms it runs for some 12 miles through relatively fertile and pleasant wooded countryside so typical of the Welsh Borders: more or less following the valley of the River Teme. There were no major engineering works on this length which was maybe as well in view of what was to come beyond Knighton an important market town. In connection with Knighton a story must be told against myself for on a photographic safari to the area I had an excellent 'pub' lunch between trains and then dropped into the local cattle market to see how prices compared with Ayrshire. My first reaction was that while all auctioneers were incomprehensible some were more incomprehensible than others. It took me five minutes to realise that cattle in these parts were being sold in Welsh! Luckily there was a train due shortly and I left in haste but I trust with decency. Beyond Knighton the whole character of the line changes, gone are the water meadows, gone are the trees and the relatively easy gradients, for from here to Llangunllo summit is one of the toughest stretches of line in Britain, the four miles of nearly unbroken 1 in 60 to Llangunllo Tunnel through a countryside ever bleaker. The most notable feature of this length and indeed of the whole line is the Knucklas Viaduct, not only has it a most impressive setting but is highly ornate with castellated battlements and parapets. Local lore has it that the stone that was used for its construction came from the ruins of a local castle, one of the many associated with King Arthur. Llangunllo at 980ft above sea level is the summit of the whole line and approached by a short tunnel. After this the line drops to cross the wide reaches of the upper Wye Valley before climbing to a second summit at the Sugar Loaf (820ft above sea level) followed by another tunnel and a sharp descent, much of it at 1 in 60, into the Vale of Towy crossing the curved Cynghordy Viaduct on its way. This viaduct built in a more functional style than the one at Knucklas is the other outstanding engineering feature of the line.

One of the features of the Central Wales line compared with those we have looked at before in this book is that it was very much a local effort, being built by four separate companies backed by local capital and by local engineers, notably a Mr Robertson and a Mr Watson none of the big names in early railway engineering having anything to do with it. As usual with such ventures costs and completion dates went wildly awry, and the LNW ever with an eye on the Welsh coal-fields were quick to come forward with aid, cash and ultimately absorbtion. For many years it must have been a great asset to them and was busy and prosperous, indeed even in the last few weeks of the through freight service there were four or five goods trains each way per day and they were heavy trains at that. There was one very interesting facet of these goods workings, in that the loads the drivers were willing to take up the four miles of 1 in 60 to the Llangunllo Tunnel were far in excess of those handled without a banker by the inevitable 8Fs than anywhere else I know of in the country. The sound of an 8F attacking the last mile to the Llangunllo Tunnel was something to be remembered for a long time. This in brief concludes a look at the LNW's Welsh incursions, all of them lines of character and all very different from each other, or for that matter most of the rest of the LNW's system.

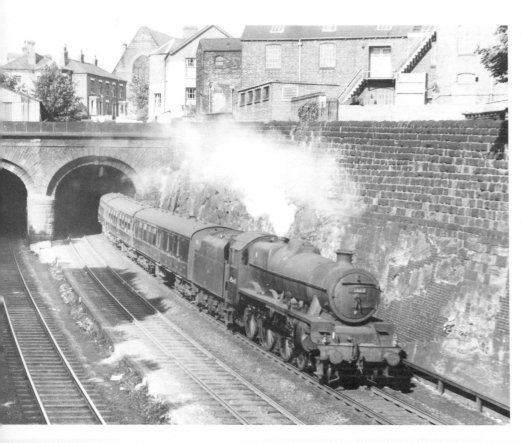

Left: Possibly the most famous 'Jubilee' of them all, No 45660 *Rooke* passes under the remains of the old city wall west of Chester station with a Birkenhead-Birmingham train in August 1962, at a time when LMR locomotives were being used to an increasing extent on the Chester-Shrewsbury section of the ex-GWR.

Below: An evening stopping train from Rhyl to Chester near Crane Street signalbox, seen in the background. The loco rather unusually for the North Wales area is one of the Standard Class 2 Moguls No 78033. This tender first view shows their Ivatt parentage very well.

Above right: The bridge that nearly disgraced Robert Stephenson. Standard No 75010 crosses the Dee Viaduct between Chester and Saltney Junction with a Crewe-Llandudno relief train on 12 August 1962. It was the collapse of the original bridge at this place that cast doubt on Stephenson's design and also more far reachingly on the use of cast iron for major bridge spans.

Below right: Another view of the Dee Viaduct with Stanier 2-6-4T No 42108 on an evening stopping train from Chester to Rhyl. The attractive skyline of the City of Chester stands out well in the evening sun while between the bridge and town is the local racecourse with the extraordinary name of the Roodee.

Top left: One of the Standard Class 5 4-6-0s No 73136 fitted with Caprotti valvegear nears Saltney Junction with a Manchester-Llandudno express on 27 June 1962. These Caprotti Standard 5s were something of an enigma; some sheds, notably Longsight (Manchester) and Balornock (Glasgow) getting excellent work out of them, while others could make nothing of them.

Centre left: The Lancashire and Yorkshire 0-6-0s were remarkably long lived machines. As late as the autumn of 1950 one of them, No 52356, still lettered LMS on the tender, trundles a long goods train over Flint troughs west of Chester, presumably heading for Saltney Yard.

Bottom left: Having laid the first set of watertroughs in the world the Chester & Holyhead line was remarkably well supplied with them. 8F No 48558 takes water from the troughs at Prestatyn with an up permanent way train in August 1962. The distinctive 'X' signboard (illuminated at night) denoting the start of the troughs for down trains is shown on the left side of this picture.

Top right: After the war when he was CME prior to Nationalisation, H. G. Ivatt made several experimental changes to the final batches of the immortal Stanier 'Black 5s'. These included roller bearings, Caprotti valve gear and in one case Stephenson valve gear. So sound was the original design that none of these modifications proved much advantage, other than the single loco with the Stephenson gear which was reckoned to be the flower of the flock. One of the rarer experiments in 'Black 5' evolution with roller bearings, Caprotti valvegear, and a double chimney pulls out of Prestatyn on 8 August 1962 with a London-Llandudno train. No 44686 is the loco one of two similarly treated.

Centre right: The most important station between Chester and Holyhead was undoubtedly Llandudno Junction. In May 1960 the Llandudno portion of the down 'Welshman' approaches Llandudno Junction with 5XP No 45586 *Mysore* in charge. The line in the foreground bearing off to the right hand side in this picture is the Conway Valley Branch the only branch line off the Chester & Holyhead still extant in 1979.

Bottom right: It was only after the war that Stanier Pacifics made regular appearances on the North Wales main line. In August 1960 'Princess' class No 46209 *Princess Beatrice* pulls out of Llandudno Junction with an afternoon train from Holyhead to Crewe. In the foreground rebuilt 'Patriot' No 45529 *Stephenson* approaches with the Holyhead portion of the down 'Welshman'.

Above left: The Stanier Moguls were never easy engines to catch, at least in daylight but one of their regular stamping grounds was the North Wales line, especially at summer weekends. On 10 August 1960 No 42976 restarts a Llandudno-Liverpool extra from Llandudno Junction.

Left: An evening photo taken from the high and typically LNW signalbox at the west end of Llandudno Junction shows a dmu coming off the branch to Llandudno Town, the main line to Holyhead bears away to the left with the outlines of Conway Castle and the tubular bridge just visible in the background.

Above: Ivatt 2MT No 46447 approaches the junction with a short pick up goods train from Llandudno Town on 10 August 1960 while a dmu for Llandudno pulls out from the junction. There was a very convenient hotel in the 'V' of this junction, the bathroom window of which proved to be an excellent vantage point for traffic coming off the branch, which I used on many occasions much to the annoyance of my fellow residents.

Right: A Llandudno-Blaenau Ffestiniog dmu leaving the beautifully situated Betws-y-Coed station in the beautiful Conway Valley in August 1960. In one of the sidings is a Pullman car that had been converted to a Camping Coach much in demand for visitors to this lovely part of North Wales.

Above: The daily goods from Llandudno Junction arrives in the moon-like landscape of spoil from the many slate quarries round Blaenau in 1960 with Ivatt Class 2, 2-6-2T No 41228 in charge. The branch still boasts a goods service which is continued to Trawsfynydd on the ex-Cambrian branch from Bala to serve the nuclear power station there.

Left: Britannia No 70026 bursts out of the Conway Tubular bridge with a Crewe-Holyhead parcels train in August 1964. The ornate portals of the bridge being designed to harmonise with the neighbouring Conway Castle. No 70026 *Polar Star* was one of the class allocated to the Western Region before being displaced by diesels and transferred north.

Above right: The down Irish Day Mail skirting the base of Conway Castle on 10 August 1960 hauled by rebuilt 'Scot' No 46156 *The South Wales Borderer*. The tracks of Conways small goods yard can be seen between the main line and the castle walls.

Right: Class 5 No 45270 passes under the city wall of Conway with an up container special from Holyhead. The wall was raised to form the arch over the railway and Conway station is just visible through the arch.

Above left: One of the features of the North
Wales railway scene in the early 1960s were
'Land Cruises' from Chester or some of the
larger holiday resorts. These trains went by
way of Ruabon and Barmouth, then along
part of the Cambrian Coast to Afon Wen,
returning to Caernarvon and the North Wales
main line. On 10 August 1960 one of these
trains is seen near Penmaenmawr hauled
rather surprisingly by Ivatt 2MT No 41234.

Left: Train 1D31, the 11.11 Manchester-
Holyhead passing the very overgrown site of
Bethesda Junction on 23 July 1977 hauled
by Class 40 No 40.001. This junction a mile
east of Bangor originally was for a short
branch to Bethesda and was one of the first
lines in the area to close.   *David M. Cross*

Above. The Britannia tubular bridge in all its
glory before being seriously damaged by fire
and extensively rebuilt. Standard 4MT
No 75011 emerges from one of the twin
tubes with a Holyhead-Crewe train on
9 August 1960, dwarfed by the ornamental
lions that were such a feature of the bridge.
Daylight is visible at the far end of the down
tube.

Right: One of the smallest, if not the smallest
of BR diesel shunters, is the 01 class of which
there were only two built. They were built by
Barclays with a Gardner engine and
mechanical transmission. Relatively low
powered they were not followed up, but had
the advantage of being exceedingly light,
weighing only 25 tons. On account of their
light weight they gravitated to Holyhead
where they were set to work carting stone to
reinforce the outer breakwater. On
27 October 1977 No 01.002 potters about
on the breakwater by which time it was the
sole survivor, the other one being
canabalised to keep it in operation.
David M. Cross

Top left: 'Western' Class 52 diesel-hydraulic D1023 *Western Fusilier* coasts across the Cheshire Plain near Nantwich with 1Z08 a Paddington-Chester enthusiasts special on 29 January 1977. While the WR diesel-hydraulics normally did not work north of Shrewsbury it was not unknown for them to work through to Crewe on ordinary service trains. *David M. Cross*

Centre left: A Birkenhead-London (Paddington) train coasting over the complex junctions at the north end of Shrewsbury station in August 1964 with Class 5 No 44713 in charge. The train is coming off the ex-GWR line from Chester and the lines from Crewe can be seen curving in ahead of the engine. It was on this curve that the LNW staged a particularly messy high speed derailment in October 1907 when the 1.20am mail from Crewe to the West of England ran on to the curve at about four times the permitted speed. Like other mysterious high speed derailments about the same time the reason has never been explained.

Bottom left: While the architecture of Shrewsbury station was very typical of the LNW it was actually a joint station with the GWR. In later years of steam the west to north trains more often than not changed engines here. This picture shows a Plymouth-Liverpool express just arrived behind 'Hall' No 4946 *Moseley Hall* while Class 5 No 45253 waits in the centre road to work the train forward.

Above right: Apart from the LNW's line from Crewe that company also had a direct link between Shrewsbury and Stafford by way of Wellington. On an August evening in 1964 Standard Class 5 No 73036 waits to leave Shrewsbury with a stopping train to Stafford, a service that has subsequently been withdrawn.

Right: The immaculately restored 'Princess Royal' Pacific No 6201 *Princess Elizabeth* passing Coleham Junction on 26 April 1976 with the M&GN Societies 'Inter City' steam hauled from Newport to Chester. The lines diverging to the right are the start of the Cambrian Railway's track to the west Wales coast. In steam days this was also the site of Coleham Shed. *David M. Cross*

Left: Of all the many attractive stretches of line between Shrewsbury and Hereford undoubtedly the most scenic was the few miles on either side of Church Stretton. In this 1964 photo 5XP No 45660 *Rooke* tops Church Stretton summit with the mid-morning Shrewsbury-Swansea train via the Central Wales line.

Below: 8F No 48706 coasts down from Church Stretton to Craven Arms with a southbound goods in June 1964. By the make up of the train it was probably bound for Hereford but could have been for the Central Wales line as the 8Fs were used on either road.

Bottom: The 'Jointness' of the Shrewsbury-Hereford line is illustrated by this photo near Church Stretton on 24 April 1964. A Liverpool-Plymouth express drops down towards Craven Arms with WR 'Warship' diesel-hydraulic D860 *Victorious* in charge.

Right: 8F No 48409 climbing the final mile of 1 in 112 to Church Stretton summit on 24 April 1964. The train is mainly composed of cattle wagons, something no longer seen on BR today. No doubt this will be from the Central Wales line taking cattle from the hill country to the great spring market at Shrewsbury.

Below: A Manchester-Swansea (via Cardiff) train immediately south of Craven Arms on 5 June 1964 hauled by class 47 D1563 in the two tone green livery that suited these engines, breaking up their 'biscuit box' lines. The station in the background and clutches of GWR style lower quadrant signals that were so much a feature of Craven Arms 15 years ago have vanished without trace.

Above: Diesel in disgrace. 'Warship' No D838 *Rapid* making a not so rapid approach to Craven Arms with a Plymouth-Liverpool express on 5 June 1964. The diesel had got to Hereford in an ailing condition and Hereford's station pilot 'Castle' No 5000 *Launceston Castle* had been summoned to assist to Shrewsbury. The fact that it was a 'Castle' that was 'spare' at Hereford was fortuitous as so 'joint' were the workings on this line that it could equally well have been a 'Black 5'.

Left: 'Britannia' No 70025 *Western Star* recovering from a signal check at Craven Arms with a Morecambe-Weymouth pigeon special in June 1964. Though originally allocated to Canton shed (Cardiff) by this time the loco had been transferred to Crewe, but there is no doubt that some of the best work the WR got out of their 'Britannias' was on the north to west route through Hereford.

Above: A week before all through freight services over the Central Wales line were withdrawn, 8F No 48761 rounds the sharp curve to join the Shrewsbury and Hereford line at Craven Arms on 5 June 1964. The length of train is typical of the heavy goods traffic worked over the line right to the end of steam and goods traffic.

Right: Just as Shrewsbury was normally the northern limit of Western engine working so Hereford was the change over point for LMR locos that had worked through from Crewe and the north. On 27 June 1962 a southbound parcels approaches Hereford behind Class 5 No 44814 of Saltley Depot in Birmingham. This and the cleanliness of the locomotive indicate that it was probably being 'run-in' after an overhaul at Crewe, the north to west route being popular for such duties.

Above: Apart from the LNW having a finger in the Hereford pie, the Midland also had an isolated branch that ultimately got to Brecon by kind permission of the LNW on one hand and the Cambrian on the other. This 1962 picture shows Ivatt 2-6-0 No 46518 setting off for Brecon with an afternoon train at the north end of Hereford station.

Left: One of the most attractive parts of the Central Wales line was between Knighton and Bucknall where the line followed the thickly wooded valley of the River Teme which at this point is also the border between England and Wales. On the second last day of steam hauled passenger services over the line, 12 June 1964, Class 5 No 45272 nears Bucknall with a Swansea-Shrewsbury train.

Above right: The first town of importance on the Central Wales line west of Craven Arms was Knighton, at one time the terminus of the line. In steam days this was a station of some importance for here the easy grades of the Teme valley gave way to the arduous climb to Llangunllo and not only was it a station for banking engines, but often for remarshalling trains as well. On 5 June 1964 the morning Swansea-Shrewsbury train takes water at Knighton with Class 5 No 45190 in charge.

Right: The wooden station at Knucklas was primitive in the extreme and unique to the line. It had no goods yard and was little more than a halt. On 12 June 1964 8F No 48328 passes Knucklas with the thrice weekly pick-up goods to Llandrindod Wells with a glorious backdrop of the upper Teme Valley.

Above left: Another view of the unique Knucklas station in June 1964 as Standard Class 5 No 73097 passes slowly by in case of custom, as by this time trains stopped by request. They were not often asked to do so but had to slow down just in case. The Knucklas Viaduct dominates the middle distance.

Left: If Knucklas station was plain the viaduct more than made up for this, with its castellated portals and parapets. Built in local stone reputedly from one of King Arthur's many castles, it makes an impressive setting for Standard 4MT No 80069 with a Shrewsbury-Swansea train on 5 June 1964.

Above: On a sparkling June morning in 1964 5XP No 45577 *Bengal* makes light work of the 1 in 60 climb from Knucklas to Llangunllo tunnel with the mid-morning Shrewsbury-Swansea train. The cleanliness of the loco is a tribute to the spirit of Coleham Shed (Shrewsbury) for when I enquired the previous evening what was to be on this train I was told they would 'run a rag' over her for me.

Right: The same spot between Knucklas and Llangunllo summit the previous week finds 8F No 48739 working all out with a heavy Swansea bound freight. As I mentioned in my introduction to this section the Central Wales drivers got work out of their 8Fs unsurpassed on any other line in the country. An 8F faced with the somewhat easier climb to Shap with this load would have been whistling for a banker long before Dillicar!

Left: Standard Class 5 No 73090 shuts off as it curves round the rocky bluff prior to stopping at Llangunllo station with a Swansea-Shrewsbury train in June 1964, 10 days before steam working ceased over the Central Wales.

Below: Class 5 No 45406 bursts out of the Llangunllo tunnel with a Shrewsbury-Swansea train on 5 June 1964. It was on this occasion that I was given a wholly unexpected lunch by the signalman whose hobby between trains was cooking, an art he was exceedingly good at and insisted that passing shepherds, or train photographers, sample!

North Lancashire

I am treating this area separately from the other sections in this book as while it is limited geographically and has no outstanding natural features its history is amongst the most complex, and acrimonious, of the whole West Coast route from London to Carlisle. Technically it should have started from Parkside Junction on the Liverpool & Manchester line where our impecunious friend the Wigan branch railway began, but I have covered this in the section on the Grand Junction. The part of the country I am now considering is between Wigan and Carnforth with its various ramifications to Blackpool, Fleetwood and Heysham. Historically even today's West Coast main line was made up north of Wigan by three companies, the North Union from Wigan to Preston the Lancaster & Preston Junction Railway and the southern tip of the Lancaster & Carlisle. Sounds simple but add to this such other small companies as the Preston & Wyre and the Little North Western and confusion becomes more confounded. None of these companies appeared to be on good terms with any other and in addition the Lancaster Canal Company made life very difficult for the Lancaster & Preston Junction by buying up shares then invoking Acts of Parliament to try and bankrupt it. Luckily the amalgamation of the London & Birmingham and Grand Junction in 1846 had formed the strong nucleus of the LNW that was able thereafter to wave the big stick at the fractious companies north of Wigan.

Looking at the physical characteristics of these lines in detail. The Wigan-Preston line though only 15 miles long provided the steepest gradient so far northwards from London, with an initial climb of 1 in 104 from Wigan to Boars Head followed by an easier climb for the final 2 miles to Coppull, thereafter the line descended on broken grades to the crossing of the Ribble south of Preston near what are now Ribble Sidings. Earthworks were relatively severe with many cuttings and lengthy embankments, though no major engineering structures until the Ribble Viaduct at Preston. The North Union (Wigan/Preston) had as its engineer one of the near greats of early railway engineering, Vignoles: an eccentric near genius, whose ideas poured out on the railway scene like water from a burst dam. There is no doubt that Vignoles had several very good ideas, but never worked on one long enough to develop it before going on to another. The North Union found this to their chagrin as while the route he surveyed was logical and sound, his estimates were hopelessly vague, and to make matters worse he was never there to see his plans put into effect having dashed off to nuture some other scheme in some other part of the country. Costs rose, directors fumed and Vignoles put in an appearance from time to time preferably when there were no directors about. Still the North Union was built and opened for business in 1838, the great bridge across the Ribble included. Having little stock of its own and very underpowered locomotives even for the period, it relied heavily on the goodwill of it neighbours such as the Liverpool & Manchester and Grand Junction though the two latter companies must have found it an almighty pain in the neck at times. Possibly its main claim to fame is that it was the only part of the main line to Scotland that neither Joseph Locke nor Robert Stephenson were involved with in some form or another.

While this reprobate among railways was being built, thrown together might be a better term, further seeds of dissension were being sown north of Preston in the form of the Lancaster & Preston Junction Railway. This line running through some of the easiest country between London and Carlisle was on the face of it a Locke line, however it is doubtful how much of his attention Locke gave to it personally, his eyes already being on the great hills north of Lancaster. Certainly unlike most of Locke's other lines in Britain the original estimates were wildly inaccurate which indicates that Locke delegated too much responsibility. It had the distinction in its early days of having both its terminal stations in the wrong places. Owing to differences of opinion with the North Union there were two stations in Preston, though to be sure they were connected but such was the squabbling about who ran the connection that it was for a long time little used. The Lancaster & Preston was built on a shoe string and having vastly exceeded its estimates was impecunious from the word go. The irony of this being that it is probably the most intensively used double track section of the London-Carlisle line today and as soon as the Lancaster & Carlisle came into being: and the LNW managed to knock some semblance of sense into the feuding heads of its directors and their neighbours it became a very profitable railway indeed. Physically it is a line without interest being nearly straight with no major earthworks or engineering features, apart from an easy climb for $1\frac{1}{2}$ miles out of Preston and a sharp drop of half a mile into Lancaster it is as near level throughout as makes no matter.

Before leaving Preston another railway that was to become jointly owned (with the Lancashire & Yorkshire) must be considered. This was the Preston & Wyre Railway, again a line of little interest scenically running across the flatlands of the Wyre peninsular to Fleetwood. This line however has two claims to fame, the first that through the port of Fleetwood it formed part of the first all steam route between London and Glasgow. Opened in 1839 allowing for the usual incredible complications round Preston there was a through railway between Euston and Fleetwood. From there to Ardrossan a steamer aptly named the *Fire King* formed a sea link while the G&SW provided a service between Ardrossan and Glasgow taking some 25 hours throughout. Still it was infinitely more comfortable and in winter probably more reliable than the old stage coach routes over Shap and Beattock. Indeed this service lasted for some years after the railway was opened throughout between Preston and Glasgow. The Preston & Wyre Railway's other claim to fame must be the creation of the holiday complex of Blackpool and Lytham, the potentials of which were not long in being recognised by the two railways concerned. It was a case of the holiday possibilities of the North Wales coasts

being repeated, and at a place very much nearer the heart of industrial Lancashire. Apart from a steady mineral traffic to and from Wyre Dock, mainly coal to Ireland, the complex of lines that grew up in the Blackpool area very soon eclipsed Fleetwood in railway importance and even to this day at times such as the Northern Wakes weeks, Glasgow Fair holidays and Blackpool illuminations the Blackpool area sees more than its fair share of excursions. The key to this web of lines to Lytham, Blackpool and Fleetwood was the junction at Kirkham now very much reduced in status but at one time handling a prodigous traffic at peak periods. By the same token various lines that were part of the Lancashire & Yorkshire fed into Preston from the east making it a focal point for many of the lines in north Lancashire. Luckily by the time traffic really built up the various feuding parties, under threats from the LNW had agreed on a joint station, not a very good one it must be admitted; as it is still the major cause of delay to the West Coast expresses today, but it was at least one station served by all the lines involved.

While the number of railways in the Lancaster area was nothing like as complex as that around Preston the ownership, especially in early days was. The Lancaster & Preston Junction terminated at a station nearer to the city than the present day Castle station and which was used for some time as a goods station. The embryo Lancaster & Carlisle for a long time could not make up its mind where to have either its line or its station. To make confusion worse the Little North Western built a line down the Lune Valley and on to Morecambe and ultimately Heysham Harbour had its own station at Green Ayre, well below the levels contemplated by the Lancaster & Preston Junction or the L&C. Once the final decision to build the Lancaster & Carlisle over Shap was decided, the details of which I will discuss in the next section, it became obvious that the L&C station would have to be on a high level with a high viaduct across the Lune. The site of the present Lancaster Castle station was chosen but this entailed what has become one of the scourges of the West Coast main line ever since, Lancaster Old Junction where the new extension to the Castle station and the north left the original Lancaster & Preston line on a sharp left hand curve

and equally sharp descending gradient. To this day this turnout is subjected to severe speed restrictions and seen from the cab of an electric after a sprint northwards from Preston is rather an alarming piece of railway geography. In the event Lancaster Castle station despite being built by the Carlisle Company was very LNW style in its architecture, and of all the West Coast main line stations has retained its LNW flavour to this day. The Midland subsequently built a very steeply graded spur between Green Ayre and Castle whose last through traffic ironically was the demolition trains engaged in lifting the Midlands line from Wennington to Morecambe.

Once the Lancaster & Carlisle had taken the plunge to cross the Lune on a high level the remainder of the line to Carnforth was obvious and ran through the dune country of Hest Bank on easy grades. In 1858 the Lancaster & Carlisle built a branch towards Morecambe from what is now Morecambe South Junction. The intention of this was to make use of Morecambe Harbour owned by the Little North Western as a port for the export of minerals. The take over of the Little North Western by the Midland put paid to this idea and the LNW line terminated at Morecambe (London Road) station. About the same time the L&C built a single line from Bare Lane to Hest Bank giving direct access from Morecambe to the north. Morecambe as a harbour was never much of a proposition but

Heysham some three miles to the south was, but the Midland having annexed the Little North Western were quicker on the uptake than the LNW so the extension from Morecambe to Heysham was built under Midland auspices, though there were connecting lines at Morecambe with the LNW. It is also interesting to note in passing that the Midland used the Lancaster-Morecambe section for a very early experiment in overhead electrification which survived into the 1950s.

I have gone into the history of this Lancaster-Carnforth-Morecambe triangle in some detail as the present day workings are in a sense the worst of both worlds. The Midland line down the Lune Valley is closed and lifted but their elaborate Promenade station is still open, served by trains running off the LNW by way of Morecambe South Junction and Bare Lane. The LNW London Road station is closed and demolished. Traffic to and from Heysham has to run into Promenade station, the loco run round before setting off westwards for Heysham. At the time of writing I am not certain whether Heysham Harbour is still in operation. Severe silting caused by the tides of Morecambe Bay caused it to lose the passenger service to Belfast in the early 1970s though a limited amount of freight traffic, mainly in containers, was handled in the outer harbour. One postwar branch of considerable importance was built to join the

Above: Class 8F No 48747 approaches Preston from the south with a Rose Grove-Wyre Dock coal train. In the background is the bridge over the Ribble that caused a minor fracas when the North Union was building it, as Vignolse design was suspect. However, in the event it stood for many years until the present greatly enlarged structure was built in connection with the formation of Ribble Sidings marshalling yard.

Above: A massive London-Heysham parcels train pulls out of Preston in May 1968 behind Class 50 No D402. This photo was taken from the northern most of Preston's signalboxes that controlled the great gantry seen in the background.

Morecambe-Heysham line to serve the new oil refinery at Heysham Moss and generated a considerable traffic for a few years, though this too is on the wane as the constantly shifting sands of the bay make it impossible for deep draught tankers to unload at the refinery any longer. The most important line into Morecambe today is the $1\frac{1}{2}$ miles of single track between Hest Bank and Bare Lane, for this not only carries all the oil and freight traffic to the north but also the Leeds-Morecambe service that now runs by Wennington Junction and Carnforth rather than direct down the Lune Valley.

The final focal point of north Lancashire is undoubtedly Carnforth. It was here that the Furness lines left the LNW and also a joint Midland and Furness Line from Wennington Junction crossed the Lancaster & Carlisle then threw a sharply curved spur to join the Furness platforms in Carnforth station. Relations between the LNW and the Furness were on the whole coldly polite

though they did cooperate in the matter of connections at Carnforth, much as they may have fought in the wilds of West Cumberland. The irony nowadays is that while the Furness side of Carnforth remains and prospers, mainly thanks to the privately owned 'Steamtown Museum', the LNW side of the station is closed and demolished. Aesthetically this is no loss as it was one of the dullest, coldest darkest places I can remember, and this on the Lancaster and Carlisle line is no mean tribute to anyone who remembers Oxenholme in a north-west wind or Tebay in winter. Stations were not the L&Cs strong point . . . not only did they tend to look like prisons but in many cases must have felt like one. I have carried this section on north Lancashire as far as Carnforth for while strictly speaking on the Lancaster & Carlisle it is the last of the many complex junctions in that part of the country. It is also the end of the plains for from here on the West Coast route faces the hills all the way to Carlisle.

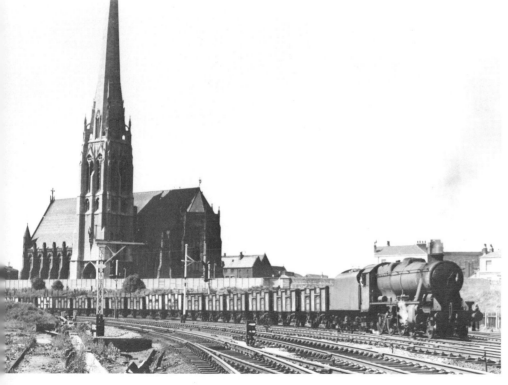

Above: The signal gantry at the north end of Preston station was one of the last, if not the very last semaphore signal gantries in Britain, surviving right up until the Crewe-Glasgow electrification and its attendant re-signalling. This battery of signals forms an impressive background to Class 5 No 45095 getting to grips with a Ribble Sidings-Heysham goods on 10 June 1968.

Left: 8F No 48247 approaches Preston off the Blackpool lines on 10 June 1968 with a train of empty coal wagons from Wyre Dock to Rose Grove. In the background is the church, with the impressive spire, the top of which is reputed to be solid, but for all that, is still very much a part of the Preston railway scenery. In the foreground on the lefthand side is the remains of the Preston Loco shed in the process of demolition.

Above: One of the more surprising features of Preston was the Preston Dock branch that emerged into the middle of the station complex like a rabbit burrow. In this 1968 photo No D312 emerges from the tunnel from Preston Dock with a goods for Ribble Sidings. The main station is on the right of the photo, and some idea of the steepness of the branch is given by the retaining walls on either side of the branch.

Below: Train 1Z68, an excursion from Wellingborough to Blackpool for the illuminations passes Kirkham on 18 October 1976 hauled by No 45.066. A class of locomotive not common on the West Coast lines. *David M. Cross*

Above right: Train 1A67 the 12.20 Blackpool-Euston express passing Kirkham on 18 October 1975 with Class 50

No 50.029 in charge. Kirkham is now a shadow of its former self as in the days when the lines in the Wyre peninsular were joint with the LNW and L&Y it controlled the lines to Blackpool, Lytham and Fleetwood. Of these only the direct line to Blackpool and the Fleetwood branch remain. Class 50s were used on these trains after the electrification for a short while before being transferred to the Western Region. *David M. Cross*

Right: A wet day at Garstang on 14 July 1967. So wet was it further north that I was driven to the Lancashire plains for shelter and was amply rewarded for this decision, as for some hours round midday trains passed in both directions block to block, giving me a vivid insight into the traffic density over this part of the WCML. 'Britannia' No 70032 *Tennyson* heads a Carlisle-Crewe parcels. This photo gives a good idea of the country that the Lancaster and Preston line passed through which makes the wildly inaccurate original estimates for building the line all the more surprising.

Left: Another 'Britannia' No 70031 *Byron* near Garstang with a northbound goods on 14 July 1967. The train is on the site of the former Brock watertroughs where the line runs adjacent to the M6 motorway. While both the engines in these pictures are named after poets I doubt if either could have waxed elequent on the beauties of the scenery between Lancaster and Preston.

Below: A lightly loaded Freightliner from Willesden to Glasgow sweeps through Lancaster Castle station on 20 August 1974 behind No 85.037. Despite the all purpose plastic canopy above the platform, Lancaster still retains more of the L&C/LNW type of architecture than many stations on this line.

Right: The 'singing bridge' of Lancaster may lack the baroque grandeur of the Bridge of Sighs in Venice but it is interesting none the less. When the Lancaster & Carlisle line linked with the Lancaster & Preston Junction Railway, Locke was forced to bridge the Lune at a high level immediately north of the Castle station. In the early 1960s this bridge had the main spans replaced and one of the effects was that with a west wind blowing off Morecambe Bay the bridge gave out a low pitch resonance that could be heard all over the town. Class 40 No D216 *Campania* crosses the 'singing bridge' with a London-Windermere train on 10 July 1968.

Below right: On 11 July 1968 the afternoon Glasgow-Liverpool train restarts from Lancaster Castle station hauled by the doyen of the Class 50s No D400. The reason for the station's distinctive name is clearly visible on the skyline.

Left: The end of an era in more ways than one. The last Standard Class 5 in active service No 73069 waits at Lancaster (Green Ayre) station to collect a train of scrap from the demolition of the Little North Western's (ex-Midland) line down the Lune Valley. Green Ayre station visible in the background with the spur leading to the LNW line in the foreground.

Below left: Class 5 No 44897 leaves Heysham Harbour station with a short ballast train on 24 May 1968. This, the passenger side of Heysham in now completely closed owing to the harbour silting up.

Top right: A general view of the Heysham Harbour complex in May 1968 before the silting up became so bad that much of it had to be abandoned. Class 5 No 44877 pulls out with a parcels train to Leeds while the extensive goods sidings are clearly visible in the background, still busy at that time, before the capricious tides of Morecambe Bay took their toll with silt deposits.

Centre right: A Ribble Sidings, Preston-Heysham goods train entering Morecambe Promenade (ex-Midland) station, on 10 July 1968, hauled by Class 5 No 44971. The loco ran round at Morecambe before proceeding tender first to Heysham. These lines between Preston, Carnforth and Morecambe were the last stronghold of steam working in Britain.

Below: Train 4N28 the afternoon Heysham Moss-Leeds bulk oil train was a heavy one and usually double-headed. On 24 May 1968 Class 25 No D5168 pilots 9F No 92077 out of Morecambe near the site of the LNW London Road station.

Top left: Class 5 No 44874 waits at Bare Lane (Morecambe) with the breakdown train returning to Carnforth after re-railing two large bogie oil tank wagons derailed at the entrance to Morecambe station. A Morecambe-Lancaster dmu occupies the other platform. The breakdown train was halted here as the single line section to Hest Bank was occupied by a Leeds-Morecambe dmu.

Centre left: Empty oil tanks working to the refinery at Heysham Moss cross from the West Coast main line on to the single track spur to Bare Lane immediately south of Hest Bank. In this 1967 photo Class 5 No 45231 is in charge with a typical early morning mist wafting about Morecambe Bay in the background.

Below: The morning Glasgow-Birmingham express picking up water from Hest Bank troughs in April 1951. The loco is a rather grimy No 46225 *Duchess of Gloucester* still with the cut down top to the smoke box carried by some of the de-streamlined 'Duchesses' well into the middle 1950s. The mass of telegraph wires and elaborate pole to support them was typical of the old LNW lines of this epoch.

Above: The secret trial. On 22 July 1975 the classic LNW 'Jumbo' No 790 *Hardwicke* was steamed for a trial run from Carnforth to Sellafield. The previous autumn when this historic locomotive was moved from the Clapham Museum to Steamtown at Carnforth it was assumed that it would never steam again. However, all through the winter work went on, restoring the locomotive to running order, and the trial run was arranged for 22 July, which had to be the wettest day of an otherwise sunny summer. So closely guarded was this trial that I was only invited to travel on it through the good offices of the NRM at 36 hours notice and even when I got to Carnforth I still couldn't believe it possible. Still all went well and this photo in the Furness platform of Carnforth station shows *Hardwicke* ready to go, with Bill MacAlpine's preserved GE saloon in tow. Could there be any greater contrast than the 'Jumbo' in the foreground and the catenary supports on the WCML above the station roof?

Right: In my introduction to this section I described the LNW's section of Carnforth station as one of the dullest, coldest and darkest of all the Lancaster & Carlisle stations. This photo on 7 July 1968 shortly before its closure sums it all up as a Morecambe-Windermere train waits in its melancholy platforms, hauled by Class 5 No 45268 deputising for a dmu which had failed.

Above: Standard Class 4 No 75021 leaves the south end of Carnforth yard on 14 July 1967 with a parcels train for Heysham. These Standard 4, 4-6-0s, though late comers to the north were very well received and put in some excellent work especially in view of the fact that the end of steam was nigh and maintenance was minimal.

Below: The classic 'Black 5' with all the aristocratic elegance of Staniers art displayed in full in the finish which they originally must have sported. An open day at 'Steamtown' on 20 August 1974 finds 'Black 5s' Nos 44932, 45407 and 44871 lined up in bright array. I say 'Black 5s' but this is not strictly correct as No 44932 was in the experimental green livery tried on her after Nationalisation for appraisal by the Board. It

was a strange shade being half way between the GWR drab waterlogged marsh shade and the Southern's rather vulgar malachite. Luckily it was not perpetuated, as in my opinion if engines cannot be black, they should at least be red. There was one glorious exception and this was the true Caledonian blue which we shall meet in the final section of this book.

Cumbria

The final section of this book is devoted to the great main line of the Lancaster & Carlisle and its various branches. So far in this book I have been considering lines constructed through relatively level country, with the exception of the Cental Wales. However there is a wealth of difference between the Central Wales and the Lancaster & Carlisle. The former grew up in bits and pieces at a time when the steam locomotive had been proved to be able to climb hills, and though it ultimately became an important through route from Swansea to the north and west, it was basically a local line at heart. The L&C was not. From its inception it was to be a link between Scotland and London but when it was first mooted in 1835 the great hills between Lancaster and Carlisle looked an insurmountable obstacle. From then until 1844 when work started in earnest on the line as we know it today there were all sorts of proposals for linking Lancaster with the Border City. It is worth noting the alternative schemes in brief. The first was a line round the West Cumberland coast which was not only circuitous but entailed the building of several great embankments across Morecambe Bay and the Duddon Estuary. The strange thing about this West Cumberland route is that it was proposed by Robert Stephenson who normally considered that the shortest distance between two points was a straight line, and had no fear of tunnels despite his experience at Kilsby. A line was built roughly on this route by the Furness Railway and it is of passing interest that Stephenson's great embankment across Morecambe Bay has been revived again in recent years, not as a railway but as a barrage for converting the tides in the bay to electricity, and probably carrying a road to avoid the present long detour through Heversham.

It is as well that the main line was not carried round the coast as parts of the Furness line exposed to the westerly gales sweeping in off the Irish Sea, notably near St Bees Head have given endless trouble over the years with slips and storm damage. The other two alternatives proposed in the early days where a line up the Lune Valley to Tebay then a tunnel under Orton Scar into the Eden Valley near Appleby and on to Carlisle, on what was to become the Settle & Carlisle line 30 years later. The third proposal and to my mind the best was by way of Kendal and up Longsleddale, then a tunnel under the Gatescarth Pass, along the western side of Haweswater and then down the valley of the Lowther to Penrith. This route would have been the same at its southern and northern ends as the main line today. There are various explanations of why it was not adopted, all of them contradictory but possibly all containing a grain of truth. Certain parties in Kendal didn't want it, assuming that the smoke from the locomotives would spoil the water needed for what was then a very prosperous weaving industry. Wordsworth undoubtedly thought it would kill the daffodils he was always writing odes to. Locke hated tunnels, and after Woodhead on the Great Central who could blame him. In the end the present route was a compromise that really satisfied nobody other than railway enthusiasts to whom Shap became a mecca. The line as built ran through relatively easy country to Hincaster where the first great climb to Grayrigg began. It was in every way a 'Locke' line in so far as he used every possible contour of the landscape to avoid too severe grades or too many earthworks. The first result of this was that the line was carried on the flank of the hills east of Kendal through Oxenholme, this promptly infuriated the citizenry of Kendal who demanded, and got, a branch. Once over the first summit at Grayrigg the line headed more or less on a level course through the Lune Gorge with remarkably enough a mile of straight track known to the Carlisle and Tebay drivers as the 'Fair Mile'. This length through the Lune Valley as far as Tebay was much as proposed for the Lune Valley-Orton-Appleby scheme. However at Tebay the Lancaster &

Above: The transition from the plains of north Lancashire and the hills of Shap is not as abrupt as many people think, for though the hills are visible all round, the WCML between Carnforth and Oxenholme runs through pleasant pastoral rolling country. This photo of Class 86 No 86.018 heading southwards near Burton and Holme gives a good impression of the landscape between Carnforth and Oxenholme.

Carlisle swung westwards to climb over Shap Fell before following the valley of the River Leith to Penrith. From there to Carlisle the route was down the Petterill Valley to Carlisle as proposed for the Gatescarth Pass line.

It is easy in retrospect to criticise this line, but when considered with the facilities available at the time it was a very logical compromise, even if over the years the need for assisting engines on Grayrigg and Shap Banks must have been a costly procedure. Both the other routes would have required infinitely greater earthworks than the Shap line, also tunnels. One can scoff at Locke's dislike of such things but it has to be remembered that in the 1840s dynamite had not been invented and the only form of explosive available was 'black powder' a notoriously fickle and ineffectual means of blasting through rock. So the great main line across the fells came into being. One other point is worth noting, and that was the fact that Locke had far more faith in the steam locomotive than any other contemporary engineers. The idea of four miles at 1 in 75 would have shocked Stephenson and scared Brunel out of his wits. There is a story that Locke did take an interest in steam locomotive design at one stage in his career but this cannot be substantiated, Brunel likewise tried his hand in the locomotive realm with disastrous results that poor Daniel Gooch had to try to make work, a task that was beyond even Gooch's genius. In my introduction to this book I mentioned that it was the fire throwing black engines of the LNW that fascinated overseas railway enthusiasts more than anything else in Britain. As I know to my cost since returning home from working abroad, of all the railways in this country that visitors from the Antipodes or America wanted to see

towards the end of steam it was Shap. Shap had a mystique of its own. Granted it was superbly photogenic, it was probably the first main line railway in the world to tackle a range of hills with a summit of 916ft, a poor thing by international standards that were to follow. The short sharp harsh name Shap somehow summed up the fell country of Westmorland in winter and it finally laid to rest any lingering doubts in people's minds about the power of steam.

Perhaps part of the glamour and mystique of Shap is the abrupt transition from the industrial landscapes of north Lancashire, along the sand dunes at Hest Bank then a few miles of rolling country to Oxenholme. Here the whole landscape changes as the hills close in and glimpses of Kendal in the valley below makes one realise that the line is not only climbing but has already climbed a hundred or so feet in an unobtrusive manner. Grey stone walls replace the hedges of the Midlands, grey stone houses replace the brick of Lancashire, sheep replace people. The Lancaster & Carlisle is remarkable in its contrasts for while the high hills are never far away the line never goes through them. Even Shap Summit, bleak though it may be, is in a saddle between the high limestone hills to the east and the higher, gaunter, granites to the west. Only for the last four miles from Tebay to the top is the line really on the open moorland. This raises another interesting point about the lines that Locke built for the various constituents of the West Coast route between Birmingham and Aberdeen: they have been remarkably free of snow trouble. Beattock experiences less snow blockages than the lower Nith Valley line to the west, Shap apart from the summit cutting is virtually snow free unlike the

Settle & Carlisle to the east. It is an interesting point, was it accidental, or did Locke deliberately try and minimise his cuttings to avoid the possibility of snow drifts? My own feeling is that Locke's use of the landforms had more than a little to do with this freedom from snow. There is a parallel here with sheep, which tend to follow the contours while gaining height even if it means going round the head of a gully rather than down and across it. When it comes to using the line of least resistance sheep are far more intelligent than they are given credit for, and it is seldom that a sheep track in regular use ever ends in a snow drift.

Once over the summit the landscape very quickly becomes more placid as the valleys of the Leith and Petterill are followed to Carlisle. Whereas none of the grades on this length is steeper than 1 in 125 they are a great deal longer, and many of the Carlisle crews have told me that it is the southbound approach to Shap that is the killer, especially with a 'cold' engine that has taken over at Citadel, or one whose fire has not been well maintained north of the border. Added to which coming from the south there is the level stretch from Grayrigg to Tebay for a 'breather'. The mountain section of the Lancaster & Carlisle is remarkably free of major engineering works, three short viaducts between Oxenholme and Shap and no tunnels at all. The two major works are both immediately south of Penrith over the Rivers Eamont and Lowther, these are both high graceful structures built of the local stone. Turning from this very remarkable main line to some of the branches; the first is from Oxenholme to Windermere that positively flattened acres of Wordsworth's daffodils and incensed the poet mightily. This line which terminated high above the lake posed few difficulties in construction and while once a very busy double tracked line has now fallen on evil days and is single track with Kendal the only intermediate station. While still used for occasional excursions the basic services are all dmu operated from Lancaster or Oxenholme, the great days of the 'Lakes Express' are no more.

While in the Oxenholme area one other branch is worth mentioning though it was not strictly speaking part of the LNW at all. This was a short branch from Arnside on the Furness line to Hincaster Junction $1\frac{1}{2}$ miles south of Oxenholme.

At one time this Hincaster spur as it was known, was of considerable importance for iron and coke traffic between Durham and West Cumberland. With the decline of the iron industry in and around Barrow its usefulness was over and it was closed and lifted in the early 1960s. Its main claim to fame must be the unique stone and girder bridge over the River Bela and a very sharp and slippery climb past the village of Heversham. Much of the ballast for the new marshalling yards at Kingmoor (Carlisle) came over this spur in 1959/61 from a quarry on the spur at Sandside.

One of the strange things about the conquest of Shap was that of the alternatives put forward initially, parts of most of them were built after the Lancaster & Carlisle won through to the border. The Furness coast line was completed, the Gatescarth Pass line got as far as Windermere and a line was built down the Lune Valley from a junction with the L&C at Low Gill. This was one of the most attractive branches of them all though in the event it did not turn westwards to Lancaster but made an end on connection with the Little North Western at Ingleton thus giving a through route from Skipton and Yorkshire to Carlisle and the north. While it was a through route in principle for many years it was not in practice. The Little North Western was absorbed by the Midland and the Lancaster & Carlisle became part of the LNW by amalgamation in 1859. Therein lay the seeds of trouble that was ultimately to give rise to the great Settle & Carlisle line. Left to their own devices there is no doubt that the L&C and the Little North Western could have worked in harmony at a profit to both parties, but the Midland and the LNW could not, the fault in this case being entirely the LNWs. So tense were relations that at one time there were two stations at Ingleton, one at each end of the viaduct over the Greta river. It was this total non-cooperation from the LNW that forced the Midland into building the S&C, though at the 11th hour the LNW tried to talk terms, but they were too late and the lovely line down the Lune Valley from Low Gill to Ingleton remained a Cinderella all its days until it finally closed in 1964. Other branches that were associated with the Lancaster & Carlisle, but never owned by it, were the line from Darlington across the Pennines to Penrith and Tebay. The latter at one time carrying considerable coal and iron-ore traffic between Furness and north-east England. The line to Penrith produced some minor convulsions in the LNW camp over the fate of Cockermouth, Keswick & Penrith Railway. The CK&P was undoubtedly one of the most beautiful in England, cutting as it did right through the heart of the Lake District linking Penrith with Workington. Like the Central Wales it was essentially a local venture but at the time West Cumberland was a prosperous area and a good deal of railway politics were taking place there. The LNW had got hold of the key line along the coast from Whitehaven to Maryport thus cutting the Furness off from its natural ally the Maryport & Carlisle. This annexation of the Whitehaven-Maryport line was not done without some very dubious dealings by the notorious Capt Huish and provoked counter measures by both the Furness and an independent concern called the Cleator & Workington. Now this state of railway warfare in West Cumberland played into the CK&Ps hands. The LNW wanted it badly as a means of capturing traffic for the north without the aid of the Maryport & Carlisle . . . or come to that to the south, thus cutting out the Furness. With the North Eastern's branch from Darlington to Penrith things began to look different and the CK&P started the dangerous game of playing one party off against the other. In the end it fell into the LNW enclave and interestingly enough was probably the last line where LNW locomotives were employed on express trains for as late as 1950 Webb's 'Cauliflower' 0-6-0s handled almost the entire traffic on the line including the Keswick portion of the lordly 'Lakes Express'.

The Cockermouth, Keswick & Penrith was a gem scenically but contained several very severe gradients such as the climb from Threlkeld to Troutbeck. Also on account of some weak bridges west of Keswick the largest locos allowed to work between there and Workington were of Class 2 classification, though east of Keswick Class 6 and on occasions Class 7 locos were allowed. The line between Keswick and Cockermouth and Workington closed in 1966 but a passenger service worked by dmus ran between Penrith and Keswick until 1972 with an occasional goods service to the lime works at Blencow.

The whole line has now been lifted and the railway scene in north-west England is the poorer for its passing.

This leaves us with the ultimate goal of most of the lines that came to form the LNW, either by coercion or voluntary amalgamation; Carlisle. Here the Lancaster & Carlisle were at a distinct disadvantage as two other companies had got there first, notably the Maryport & Carlisle and the Newcastle & Carlisle. The former though a small company was a prosperous one and like most small people very aggressive. Both the Newcastle & Carlisle and the Maryport companies considered the Lancaster & Carlisle as an intruder and not a very welcome one at that. The two earlier companies to get to Carlisle, after some bickering did agree to a joint station that was not very convenient for either but at least was even more inconvenient for the L&C that has to cross either or both of the rival lines on the level.

Needless to say this led to a smash, and the stern rebukes of the Railway Inspectorate about the 'wild west' workings round the Border City. The arrival of the Caledonian from the north closely allied with the L&C/LNW camp made matters slightly more chaotic so the Carlisle Station Joint Committee was set up, representing all the companies working into Carlisle. Strange to say for a committee it worked and Citadel station came into being, though the Maryport & Carlisle exacted a goodly pound of flesh for some rather useless marshland (subsequently known as Bog Junction on the Carlisle goods lines) and the North Eastern having swallowed up the Newcastle & Carlisle took sulks and retained their own rather inconvenient station near what is now London Road Junction. It was as well that the Carlisle Station Joint Committee was set up when it was, as within a very short time the Midland, the North British through its acquisition of the Carlisle & Silloth line, and the Glasgow & South Western by virtue of running powers over the Caledonian from Gretna all started using the joint Citadel station. Looking at the architecture of Carlisle today the Lancaster & Carlisle/LNW influence is still obvious despite the truncation of the massive overall roof. Until recently it was a source of considerable congestion and herein lies a mystery. To the west side of the main island platform there are three carriage sidings against the wall that

originally held the overall roof. There was plenty of space for an extra through platform that would have made all the difference at peak periods but it was never built. Why it was not is one of the more mysterious chapters in railway lore. Still what were built was a series of goods lines that avoided the passenger station to the west rather on the pattern that the Grand Junction/LNW had adopted at Crewe. This idea while helping to alleviate conjestion at Citadel was never as satisfactory as at Crewe where all the goods traffic was handled by the same closely knit group of companies in one major marshalling yard. At Carlisle, while the various companies involved finally did agree to a joint passenger station, the idea of a joint goods station was beyond the pale and each company maintained its own goods depots with some very bizzare effects. The G&SW's Currock depot for instance could only be reached by courtesy of the Maryport & Carlisle. The North British yard at Dentonholme tangled with the Caledonian so while there were goods avoiding lines they were more useful for transfer traffic between various yards than for through freight working.

During World War II things got so chaotic that the line from Dentonholme Junction to Kingmoor was quadrupled, and after nationalisation, British Railways decided that enough was enough, and built a massive new marshalling yard

north of the old Caledonian locomotive depot at Kingmoor thus enabling most of the scattered yards to be closed. At the same time with the impending run down of steam, various locomotive depots were closed and the Carlisle steam allocation centred on Kingmoor or Upperby, the latter used mainly for storing surplus locomotives. With the coming of electrification a new depot has been built at Kingmoor to the west side of the line while the old steam sheds have been demolished and at the time of writing are to be developed as an industrial estate. At the same time Upperby after being one of the main bases for the WCML electrification has now become one of the most up to date carriage cleaning and maintenance depots in the country. By a strange quirk of fate it has also over the past year been host to visiting steam locomotives, that have worked in over the Settle and Carlisle line in connection with BR's revised policy of running steam excursions over certain lines during the summer. This then completes a brief sketch of the West Coast rails between Euston and Carlisle, a task that needs three volumes and not only one, but I hope that in the illustrations I may have conveyed something of this most fascinating group of lines and given a hint of the formidable men that formed them . . . undoubtedly 'Great men can do great good or else great harm'.

Above: Oxenholme old style, with 5XP No 45717 *Dauntless* heading north on 27 July 1963 with the morning Liverpool-Glasgow express. This was taken before the run down of the Windermere branch and the extension of the platforms in connection with electrification.

Top left: Oxenholme new style, with the extended platforms and removal of the complex junction at the north end of the station. Class 87 No 87.035, subsequently named *Robert Burns*, on 24 July 1976 with the morning Manchester-Glasgow train. *David M. Cross*

Centre left: One of the last regular 'Jubilee' turns over the WCML was the Friday and Saturday afternoon summer service trains, from Liverpool to Glasgow. The most regular performer on these duties was No 45698 *Mars* shown just north of Oxenholme on 31 July 1964. The loco is sporting the diagonal yellow stripe on the cab side, an indication that it was not allowed on the electrified lines south of Crewe.

Bottom left: Class 4F No 44469 passing the bay platform at Oxenholme in 1961 with a goods from Windermere and heading into the goods yard south of the station. With the coming of electrification this scene has completely changed, the station having been modernised and the track layout greatly simplified, even the typical L&C signalbox has been demolished.

Top right: Class 40 No D387 propels the empty stock of a train from Preston out of Windermere on 1 August 1968. The locomotive then rounded the train to form the fag end of what was once the 'Lakes Express' to London. The branch has now been singled and worked on the one engine in steam principle and the 'Lakes' is no more.

Centre right: Train 1S71 the Saturday afternoon Manchester-Glasgow express climbing out of Oxenholme to Peat Lane bridge with rebuilt 'Scot' No 46118 *Royal Welch Fusilier* in charge on 20 July 1962. The evocative name for the bridge derives from the days that this road was used for carting peat into Kendal from the surrounding moors.

Bottom right: A rare sight as late as 1963. A spotless Class 5 No 44834 obviously not long out of shops climbs the initial 1 in 104 of Grayrigg Bank between Oxenholme and Peat Lane bridge with a northbound goods on 26 July 1963.

Above: The evening Carlisle-London milk train coasts down the last stretch of Grayrigg Bank towards Oxenholme near Peat Lane with D306 in charge on 26 July 1963.

Left: Class 5 No 45285 makes an all out effort past the loops at Grayrigg with an afternoon Crewe-Carlisle parcels train on 28 July 1967. The reballasting of the main line in preparation for electrification is clearly visible in this photo.

Above right: One of the strange things about the Lancaster & Carlisle line was that while its main stations were grim and gaunt, some of its less important stations had a great deal of rustic charm. This photo of Grayrigg in June 1961 shows something of that charm, though by this time the station was closed. 'Jubilee' No 45698 *Mars* heads northwards with a Birmingham-Edinburgh train on 30 June 1961.

Right: Once over Grayrigg the line actually drops for a mile or so to Low Gill providing a welcome breather for hard pressed locomotives after Grayrigg Bank. 9F No 92012 coasts down towards Low Gill with a northbound fitted freight on 21 August 1964. One of the surprising things about the line over Shap, was that the immensely powerful and free running 'nines' were never used to any great extent.

Top left: The other approach to Low Gill from the Ingleton branch. Ivatt Class 4 No 43009 heads the thrice weekly pick-up goods on 21 August 1964 shortly before the line was closed. Judging by the load of this train, the closure was more than justified, even it if was one of the most photogenic of all the Cumbrian branches.

Centre left: The Lune Valley line between Low Gill and Ingleton had two remarkable engineering features, the viaducts at Low Gill and Firbank, near Sedbergh. This shot taken on 17 September 1964 shows the empty stock of the penultimate Sedbergh School special returning to Tebay across the Firbank Viaduct hauled by Class 5 No 45081 paired with the ex-LMS self weighing tender.

Bottom left: Even by 1960 the Low Gill-Ingleton branch had lost its regular passenger services. On a late evening in August 1960 a Ramblers Excursion returns from Tebay to Bradford seen here crossing the lovely curved sandstone viaduct near Low Gill with Class 5 No 45486 in charge. It would be a day to remember for many of the ramblers, as a party of them were routed from a field near Tebay by a particularly evil minded Shorthorn bull . . . much to the amusement of the Tebay signalman and myself . . . especially myself as the same bull had shown me the gate a couple of days before.

Top right: The last passenger train down the Lune Valley branch. 1T41 arrives in Sedbergh station with a school special from Tebay having connected with a train from the south, hauled by Class 5 No 45081 on 17 September 1964. At this time these school specials were the only passenger trains on the branch which was closed completely at the end of the month.

Centre right: Against a background of shower cloud over the high Fells rebuilt 'Scot' No 46128 *The Lovat Scouts* coasts through the Lune Gorge north of Low Gill on 13 July 1963 with a relief train from Glasgow to Liverpool.

Bottom right: On 22 July 1961 'Duchess' No 46234 *Duchess of Abercorn* heads the morning Glasgow-Birmingham express into the Lune Gorge south of Tebay. No 46234 was the Stanier Pacific that put up what was probably the all time weight hauling record for a British Pacific on a Crewe-Glasgow test train in February 1939.

Top left: If I was to take this photo today I would be killed; as I would be standing on the southbound carriageway of the M6! However such apparitions were still on the drawing board when 'Britannia' No 70047, the one un-named 'Britannia', heads northwards through the Lune Gorge with train 1S91 a Birmingham-Glasgow relief, in July 1963.

Centre left: The Lune Gorge in all its glory, again taken from what is now the M6, whose planners did not have to look far, as Joseph Locke had shown them the way over a 100 years before. Rebuilt 'Scot' No 46115 *Scots Guardsman* coasts southwards through the gorge with a Glasgow Fair relief to London on 13 July 1963. This engine was destined to be the last 'Royal Scot' in regular service on BR and has subsequently been preserved.

Bottom left: When Ramsbottom of the LNW laid down the first watertroughs in the world at Aber in North Wales the company realised that they were a very good idea indeed, and were not sparing in the provision of troughs on the WCML. Undoubtedly the most scenic and best known of all were those at Dillicar a mile south of Tebay in the throat of the Lune Gorge. Under a lowering sky rebuilt 'Scot' No 46121 *Highland Light Infantry* takes water at Dillicar with the morning London-Perth express in July 1951.

Top right: Dillicar troughs in winter. 'Patriot' No 45518 *Bradshaw* heads a southbound fitted freight on 8 February 1960. Despite their altitude Dillicar troughs were never subject to icing as the traffic using them was so intense.

Centre right: Summer scene at Dillicar on 18 May 1964 as 5XP No 45574 *India* takes water with train 1M21 the Saturday Glasgow-Blackpool. The spray from the pick-up scoop under the tender is clearly visible.

Bottom right: 'Put a sock on it' was the local term for a train that was piloted from Oxenholme to Shap Summit. The origin of this term is wrapped in mystery but knowing the railwaymen of the district is probably rude. On 22 July 1961 rebuilt 'Scot' No 46103 *Royal Scots Fusilier* is piloted over Dillicar troughs by Oxenholme's Stanier tank No 42613 with the morning Manchester-Glasgow express. The River Lune from which the troughs drew their water supply is visible on the left hand side of the picture.

Left: 'Black 5' No 44736 takes a run at Shap past Tebay No 1 box on 13 July 1963 with a holiday special from Blackpool-Grangemouth. With a nine-coach load the driver must have had confidence in his engine as nine up Shap was very near the limit for a 'Black 5'.

Below left: Rebuilt 'Scot' No 46145 the *Duke of Wellingtons Regiment* coasts through Tebay with the morning Manchester-Glasgow express in August 1960. The fact that the regulator is closed indicating that the train was stopping for banking assistance.

Right: Train 1K76 the Saturdays only Keswick to Crewe and Manchester restarts from Tebay station on 13 July 1963 hauled by rebuilt 'Patriot' No 45530 *Sir Frank Ree*. On the left is the relatively modern LMS built shed that replaced one that was burned down in the 1930s. The gaunt dungeon of Tebay station is visible above the second coach.

Below: Tebay shed early on a Monday morning in 1960 with most of its allocation of locomotives preparing for action. From left to right these are Fowler 4MT No 42396, Ivatt Class 2 Mogul No 46422, that was to work the thrice weekly goods to Ingleton, Fowler No 42404, Ivatt 4MT No 43011 for the pick-up goods to Penrith, and finally another Fowler 2-6-4T No 42403. The three Fowler tanks were all being got ready for banking duties between Tebay and Shap Summit.

Above: Clan 'Pacific' No 72000 *Clan Buchanan* stops on the curve between Tebay No 2 box and Loups Fell cutting for a 'blow up' and a banker on 25 September 1961, while working 1X94 an excursion from Morecambe to Glasgow returning after the Glasgow holiday weekend.

Left: A northbound goods restarts from Tebay and heads into Loups Fell cutting after picking up a banker on 21 July 1961. The banker was one of Tebay's resident Fowler 2-6-4Ts and the train engine 'Crab' No 42925. The 'Crabs' despite their L&Y/LNW ancestory were never very common on Shap, which in view of their remarkable reputation for hill climbing in Scotland is rather surprising.

Above: 'Britannia' No 70052 *Firth of Tay* makes a lot of fuss approaching the Greenholme road bridge with a Liverpool-Glasgow train on 28 July 1961. Despite a relatively light load the train is banked by one of Tebay's Fowler 2-6-4Ts which is a reflection on the poor record that the 'Britannias' had on the northern fells when it came to climbing up them.

Right: In the summer when the weekend through trains from NE England to Blackpool was being worked over Stainmore to Tebay, they were worked forward from the latter by a 2-6-4T. This in 1961 was invariably a Fowler designed engine equipped with water scoops and to cover this turn Tebay usually borrowed a specially good one from Lostock Hall or Blackpool. On 30 June 1961 one of the borrowed Fowlers No 42379 banks a northbound goods under the Greenholme road bridge at the start of the final four miles of 1 in 75 to Shap Summit.

Top left: If I have one photo of Shap that shows the fickleness of the weather and the extraordinary quality of the light it is surely this photo of 5XP No 45681 *Aboukir* approaching Scout Green. The train is 3L07 the morning Crewe-Carlisle parcels, caught in a brief moment of sunshine between what the Met Office are wont to call frequent squally showers.

Centre left: Scout Green in more placid mood. 1S42 a relief to the overnight London-Glasgow sleeper approaches Scout Green shortly after dawn on 2 August 1964 hauled by 'Jubilee' No 45716 *Swiftsure* still paired with the low sided Midland type tender that some of the 'Jubilees', especially the Scottish Region ones, kept to the end of their days.

Bottom left: Pastoral at Scout Green in August 1960 as Fowler 4F propels a permanent way train towards Shap Summit. The loco is No 44186 and the signalbox is clearly visible with its characteristic leaning chimney, which survived until electrification when the level crossing was done away with and the box bought for preservation at Sittingbourne . . . long may it last, as many were the cups of tea I enjoyed there from the men who manned it.

Above: Half way between Scout Green and Shap Summit a road led into Salterwath Farm. This was an ideal place for a lazy man to take photos as you could park on the fell and see everything for miles in each direction. In September 1951 one of the last 'Royal Scots' still not fitted with the LMS Type 2A taper boiler No 46151 *The Royal Horse Guardsman* climbs past Salterwath with a London-Glasgow train.

Below: 'Jubilee' No 45653 *Barham* storms past Salterwath with a northbound goods on 13 June 1965. Hidden by the train was a cottage built for the surfaceman on that section who in the 1950s had the distinction of keeping a pet fox. The neighbouring farmers took rather a dim view of this beast though it was a friendly animal, and on one occasion took a very kindly view of my picnic lunch.

Left: A final look at Salterwath, and one which has mystified me ever since. The loco is No 46241 *City of Edinburgh*, shorn of its streamlined casing as shown by the sloping front of the smokebox. The train is the morning Birmingham-Glasgow in July 1950. The stock is extraordinary even allowing for the fact that it was during the Glasgow Fair holidays. Just what the origin of the first two coaches was I have never found out, but by the look of them a 'Duchess' on Shap should have shaken them to pieces.

Below: Shap Wells is probably the most photogenic spot in the country from a railway point of view, and I make no apology for the photos that are to follow, only adding that with one exception they were taken in the early 1950s when steam was king, and trains were heavy. Rebuilt 'Scot' No 46165 *The Ranger* at Shap Wells in August 1952 with the morning Birmingham-Glasgow express.

Bottom: Un-named 'Patriot' No 45508, one of the first of the class to be withdrawn makes the 1 in 75 at Shap Wells look easy with a 12-coach London-Glasgow relief train in the summer of 1952.

Right: Once again Shap's dramatic lighting highlights the elegant lines of No 46212 *Duchess of Kent* coasting past Shap Wells on an April afternoon in 1950 with the up 'Midday Scot'. The loco at this time still had the combined dome and top-feed.

Below: 'Princess' No 46211 *Queen Maud* on the 1 in 75 past Shap Wells with a London-Glasgow express in July 1952. Again the locomotive has the original combined dome and top-feed, but with 15 coaches appears to make light work of the climb to Shap. The opinion of many of the Upperby (Carlisle) men was that the 'Princesses' were surer footed on the banks than the 'Duchesses'.

Bottom: Shap in its elemental fury as the experimental English Electric gas-turbine GT3 climbs past the Wells with a test train on 6 October 1962. This series of tests conducted in typical Westmorland weather proved that GT3 was no mean performer, but alas came too late to stem the tide of diesels.

Top left: 'Duchess' Pacific No 46231 *Duchess of Atholl* coasts out of the summit cutting at Shap on 28 July 1961 with the morning Glasgow-Birmingham express, the last year before diesel took over this working. The steam operated coal pusher is in operation which accounts for the plume of steam above the tender.

Centre left: Shap under snow. The morning Euston-Perth train climbs into the summit cutting with rebuilt 'Patriot' No 45512 *Bunsen* in charge on 6 February 1960. Though the fells are snow covered the railway is remarkably clear, and indeed it was exceedingly rare for Shap ever to be closed by snow.

Bottom left: One of the summer Saturday treats on Shap in the early 1960s was a midday stopping train from Oxenholme to Carlisle hauled by anything that Oxenholme had on shed, it also was often made up of a motley collection of stock. In this 1960 photo the loco is Fowler 4MT No 42322 one of Oxenholme's stud of bankers and the coaching stock is mixed to say the least.

Above: By May 1963 the morning combined Liverpool and Manchester to Glasgow train was diesel hauled, but during the summer months when the train ran in two portions the Liverpool part was still in the hands of a 'Jubilee'. No 45627 *Sierra Leone* blasts out of the cutting to Shap Summit with 1S47 Liverpool-Glasgow. The reason for the all out effort is interesting, as a Class 40 on the preceding Manchester train had made so poor a climb that the 'Jubilee' suffered a dead stand at Shap Wells' signals.

Below: The semi-regular summer relief to the 'Midday Scot' from Crewe to Glasgow approaching Shap Summit behind Class 5 No 45182. Despite a load of ten coaches the 'Black 5' was going well without any banking assistance.

Top left: Train 1M38 the afternoon Glasgow-Liverpool express passes Shap summit on 1 August 1964 hauled by Class 5 No 45055 and 5XP No 45742 *Connaught*, which along with sister engine *Kashmir* were the last two 'Jubilees' allocated to Carlisle. This train which ran on Fridays and Saturdays in the summer was also one of the last regular steam workings over the WCML south of Carlisle.

Centre left: Early in 1960 a vast new quarry was opened at Hardendale a mile south of Shap station. This was officially known as Shap Quarry and was controlled by a box of that name opened as required. The limestone from this quarry went to Ravenscraig near Glasgow for steel making. The new quarry sidings (now electrified) are in the foreground of this picture of 'Britannia' No 70006 *Robert*

Burns heading a southbound goods on a crisp August morning in 1964.

Bottom left: As I have said before while the Lancaster & Carlisle's main stations were cold gaunt affairs some of its less important ones were architectural gems. None more so than Shap with its steeply gabled roof and glass verandah. It was also beautifully kept with hanging baskets of flowers, flower beds and oil lamps polished to perfection right to the day it closed. Class 5 No 45341 coasts in with 'Lulu' the morning stopping train from Warrington to Carlisle on 21 August 1964. The odd name for this train was on account of the reporting number 1L00, but none of the men ever called it other than 'Lulu' . . . at least I think this was the spelling. But knowing the bawdy sense of humour in these hills it could well have been 'Loo-loo!'

Above: Stranger on Shap. Rebuilt 'Merchant Navy' No 35012 *United States Lines* passes Harrisons limeworks on 13 June 1964 with an RCTS special from Leeds to Carlisle, Silloth and a lot of places in between, though the 'Merchant Navy' was detached at Penrith.

Below: Rebuilt 'Royal Scot' No 46161 *Kings Own* storms up the valley of the River Leith towards Thrimby Grange loops in the summer of 1950 with the morning Perth-London express. The little river in the foreground at this time was a clear sparkling stream full of trout asking to be caught. Years later with the expansion of Harrisons limeworks a mile to the south it turned into a river of mud, though this has now been reversed; whether the trout have returned I do not know.

Top left: Among the features of the Lancaster & Carlisle line greatly altered by electrification is the layout at Clifton and Lowther. When this picture was taken in August 1963 the station, though long since closed, was still intact as was the signal box. All this has changed completely. A southbound goods hauled by an Austerity 2-8-0 waits in the loop while an excursion from Wigan to Edinburgh coasts down the 1 in 125 behind rebuilt 'Patriot' No 45531 *Sir Frederick Harrison.*

Centre left: The old at Penrith. LNER Class J21 0-6-0 No 65100 approaches Penrith in 1951 with a train from Darlington via Stainmore. The elderly 0-6-0s had a long run on this line on account of severe weight restrictions on the viaducts at Belah and Deepdale, ultimately being replaced by Ivatt Moguls and for a short while dmus.

Bottom left: The new at Penrith. 'Duchess' Pacific No 46229 *Duchess of Hamilton* approaching Penrith with the Keswick portion of the 'Lakes Express' on 3 August 1963. This was a regular Pacific working even though the load north of Oxenholme was often only three coaches, the bulk of the train going to Windermere. From Penrith to Keswick and Workington it was latterly worked by an Ivatt Class 2 Mogul but I can recall times in 1950 when a Webb 'Cauliflower' 0-6-0 took over. No 46229 is now preserved by the NRM at York.

Above right: On summer Saturdays a relief train ran ahead of the up 'Lakes Express' with portions for Manchester and Crewe. This train was always an interesting locomotive working, depending on what Upperby (Carlisle) had on hand. In July 1K76 Keswick-Crewe snakes out of Penrith station in charge of a very clean rebuilt 'Scot' No 46154 *The Hussar.*

Right: The Keswick portion of the up 'Lakes Express' passes Penrith No 3 box on 26 July 1963 hauled by Fowler 2-6-4T No 42319. The normal working for the 'Lakes Express' was an Ivatt from Workington to Penrith then one of Oxenholme's big tank engines over Shap to Oxenholme, where the train was taken over by a 'Scot' or 'Jubilee' that had worked the main portion from Windermere. It is of interest that the tank engines involved were invariably fitted with water scoops, clearly indicated by the 'breather' at the front of the tanks on No 42319.

Above: Ex-LNWR 'Super D' No 49091 pulls out of the Eamont loops at Penrith with a northbound goods in July 1951. The name 'Super D' intrigued me for a long time until I found out that it was a superheated version of a long line of LNW 0-8-0s dating back to Webb. They were strong rugged and reliable engines if slow at times. This slowness earned them the nickname between Carnforth and Carlisle of the 'Wigan Scotsmen'.

Left: The Workington and Keswick portion of the up 'Lakes Express' entering Cockermouth station behind No 46432 on 20 August 1964, with the normal weekday load of three coaches. In bygone days Cockermouth was the meeting point between the independent CK&P railway and the LNW owned lines in west Cumberland.

Above: The Keswick portion of the down 'Lakes Express' arriving at Keswick in the summer of 1964, again with No 46432 in charge. The elaborate station at Keswick, now demolished is a reminder of its glory days as a health resort in Victorian England.

Right: The hardest part of the climb from Keswick to Penrith is between Threlkeld and Troutbeck, much of it at 1 in 50. Dominated by the Saddleback ridge in the background Ivatt 2MT No 46491 tackles the last few yards to Troutbeck on Saturday 31 July 1965 with the Keswick-Crewe (SO) train.

Above: Much to the annoyance of its neighbours, the Furness and Maryport & Carlisle, the LNW held the key to the busiest part of the west Cumberland coast by owning the line between Whitehaven and Maryport. Fowler 4F No 43963 approaches Derwent Junction on the northern outskirts of Workington with a short coal train from Flimby Colliery in August 1964.

Left: Class 5 No 45226 with a Workington bound coal train is checked at Derwent Junction in 1964 while a dmu from Whitehaven to Carlisle heads north. Derwent Junction was the point where the LNW branch to Cockermouth left the coast line to Maryport.

Above: The intense industrial landscape of parts of west Cumberland is typified by this photo of 4F No 44484 on the outskirts of Workington, with a train of empty coal wagons probably for Flimby Colliery. It was in west Cumberland that the 4Fs made their last stand as they were very suitable for the short haul, heavy mineral trains over the short sharp grades in that area. Strangely the locomotive sports the diagonal yellow stripe on its cab, denoting that it was not allowed to work under the wires south of Crewe.

Right: Penrith really marks the boundary of the fell country and the more fertile arable land in the valley of the Petterill. Class 86 No 86.002 heads southwards alongside the infant River Petterill near Plumpton with 1M27, the morning Glasgow-Liverpool express on 4 June 1974.

Left: Rather surprisingly the valley of the River Petterill narrows for a few miles round Wreay four miles south of Carlisle, giving what is scenically the most attractive part of the Penrith/Carlisle length. 'Lulu', the morning stopping train from Warrington to Carlisle sweeps round the curve towards the closed station of Wreay on 31 July 1964 with 5XP No 45663 *Jervis* in charge.

Below: One of the interesting things about train 1L00 the morning Warrington-Carlisle stopping train was the variety of motive power it produced, virtually everything from a Class 5 upwards. On 18 August 1962 No 46243 *City of Lancaster* provides super power for a mundane train seen here between Plumpton and Southwaite.

Right: The south end of Carlisle's Citadel station in 1965, the last year when steam was in considerable use on summer Saturdays. A line up of light engines with No 44903 backing on to the Dundee-Blackpool train while 5XP No 45574 *India* waits to work a train over the Settle and Carlisle and on the left Class 5 No 45340 waits its turn on an extra to Morecambe.

Below: A different scene at the south end of Carlisle six years later when the principal West Coast expresses were worked by Class 50 diesel-electrics in multiple. On 2 April 1971 Class 50s Nos D400 and D443 wait to depart with 1M30, the lineal descendent of the up 'Midday Scot'. In the centre road a dmu is parked between trips to Whitehaven.

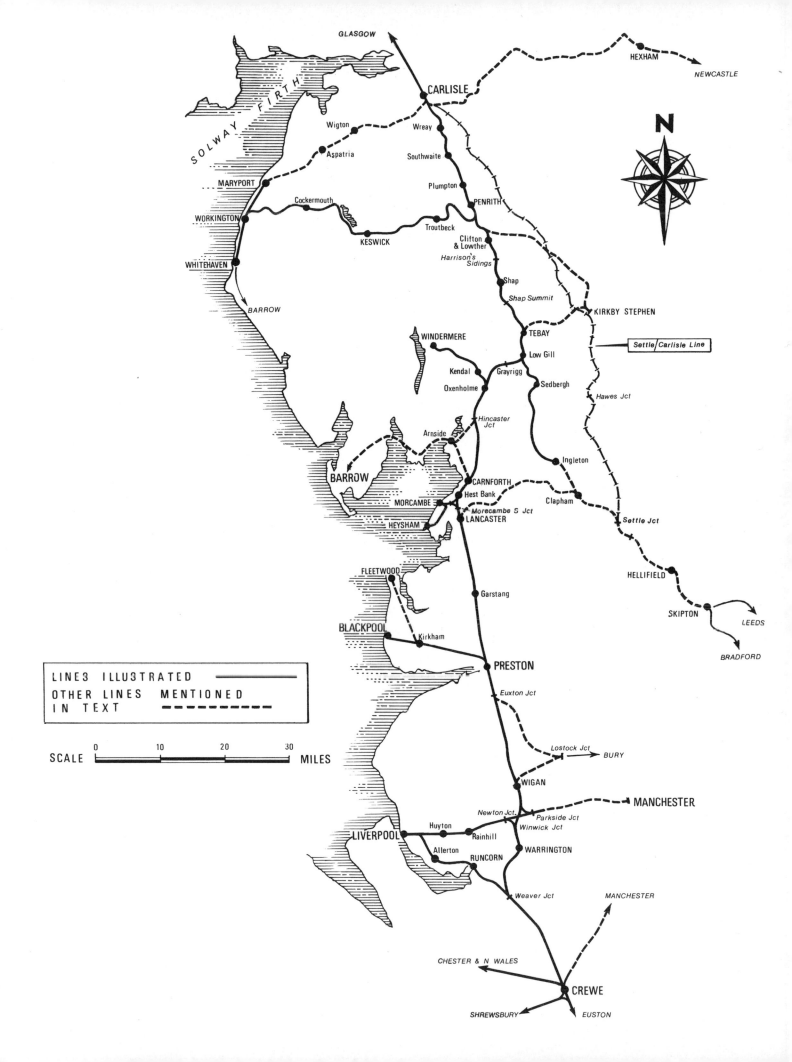

Death and transfiguration. In May 1967 Upperby Yard (*above*) is packed with condemned steam engines, among them 8Fs 48451 and 48488. *Below:* Eleven years later on 13 May 1978 steam returns to Carlisle in the form of preserved 9F No 92220 *Evening Star* hauling the 'Midland Border Venturer' from Birmingham by way of the Settle and Carlisle line.

Left: The rare sight of a freight train in Carlisle's Citadel station. On Sunday 30 August 1964 'Duchess' No 46241 *City of Edinburgh* waits at the head of a train of insulated meat containers from Broughton (Nr Biggar) and Racks (Nr Annan) to Maiden Lane (London). The reason for a goods train using the passenger station was that the avoiding lines are closed on Sundays, as apart from perishable specials such as this, there is no goods traffic through the Carlisle area.

Below left: Further motive power variations at Carlisle Citadel. For several Sundays in the summer of 1978 the electric power was cut off on the up line between Glasgow and Carlisle and all the morning expresses to the south were hauled by diesel locos with the electrics still attached with their pantographs lowered. 1M29 the Sunday morning Glasgow-Liverpool express entering Carlisle on 30 July 1978 with Class 47 No 47.553 towing No 86.253. In the background a dmu waits to work the Carlisle-Newcastle service.

Top right: The rivals at Carlisle with the impressive overall roof still intact in August 1950, giving the 'Joint' Citadel station something of the gauntness of many of the LNW's more important stations: though in fact this station was managed by a Joint Committee. The up 'Thames/Clyde Express' via the Midland route pulls out behind rebuilt 'Scot' No 46113 *Cameronian* while the up 'Royal Scot' leaves behind 'Duchess' class Pacific No 46238 *City of Carlisle*.

Centre right: Until BR gave them numbers some of the signalboxes on the goods lines avoiding Citadel station had most evocative names. On 3 November 1967 Class 47 No D1804 is seen on the complex of goods lines from Rome Street Junction signalbox. The lines to the left connect with the S&C and Newcastle routes while the sharp turnout to the right connects with the Maryport & Carlisle line. It was to avoid an excessively steep turn out that the line from Upperby took the odd looking loop that this train is on.

Bottom right: BR called it Carlisle number something or other, but to the end of its days the men called it Bog Junction: ostensibly as it was built on land reclaimed from a swamp but I feel there may have been another reason. Ivatt Class 4 Mogul No 43121 approaches Bog Junction with a transfer goods from Kingmoor Yard to Upperby.